Ideology and social welfare

Vic George
*Professor of Social Policy and
Administration and Social Work
University of Kent*

and

Paul Wilding
*Senior Lecturer in Social Administration
University College, Cardiff*

Routledge & Kegan Paul
London, Boston and Henley

First published in 1976
by Routledge & Kegan Paul Ltd
39 Store Street,
London. WC1E 7DD,
Broadway House,
Newtown Road,
Henley-on-Thames,
Oxon. RG9 1EN and
9 Park Street,
Boston, Mass. 02108, USA
Reprinted in 1978 and 1979
Set in IBM Press Roman
by Pentagon Print
and printed in Great Britain by
Redwood Burn Limited
Trowbridge & Esher
© Victor George and Paul Wilding 1976

ISBN 0 7100 8273 8 (c)
ISBN 0 7100 8290 8 (p)

CONTENTS

Introduction

The thesis of this book is that it is impossible adequately to understand the views of those who write about social welfare policy without taking account also of their social values and their social and political ideas. To illustrate this thesis, we begin with a general discussion which aims to relate theorising about social problems and social policy to more general social and political theory. We go on to discuss the views of four groups of thinkers, groups we describe as the anti-collectivists, the reluctant collectivists, the Fabian socialists and the Marxists.

Probably not all the authors whose ideas we discuss would be entirely happy about how they have been classified and described. We have tried to be fair although some of the descriptions are admittedly rather clumsy. Any grouping is likely to offend some susceptibilities. It is important to emphasise from the start that our concern in these four chapters is to depict a group position rather than to discuss in detail the work and views of individual authors. The first task clearly involves the second but our focus is the group view rather than individual views.

Any choice of authors for a discussion such as this is open to criticism. Everyone will have views about who should have been selected and who rejected. We have confined ourselves to the twentieth century and we have chosen people we considered were important and interesting, and who, in some cases, are under-considered in traditional social administration literature.

For the anti-collectivists, Hayek and Friedman chose themselves. They must be the central figures in any such group. We added Enoch Powell as a contemporary British figure whose general social and political theories are often neglected because of the emotions aroused by his more publicised political pronouncements. We refer to the work of the Institute of Economic Affairs but do not discuss it in detail. It is essentially an attempt to apply and work out the theories and insights of Hayek and Friedman.

Beveridge, of course, was an obvious first choice for the reluctant collectivists although his general political and social views have never been adequately expounded. Because of its technical complexity, Keynes's work tends to be ignored by non-economists but it has been of major importance for the development of social as well as economic policy. Galbraith expresses this point when he describes 'The General Theory', as 'the most influential book on economic and social policy so far this century'.[1] Burns clarifies exactly why this should be so. 'The economic theory of Lord Keynes', he writes, 'still stands in the minds of many as a symbol of almost everything that goes to make up the Western conception of the positive state. To a large extent it was the fountain head of that conception.'[2] We include Galbraith himself because over the years he has become increasingly concerned with social policy as, at the same time, he has become a more convinced — though still a reluctant — advocate of collectivist solutions.

The Fabian socialists are in some ways the most difficult group to write about because their views have become the orthodoxies of social administration. Their position is clear and yet the differences between, for example, Tawney and Crosland are considerable. These two, however, with the addition of Titmuss, serve as representatives of this school of thought.

The choice of authors to represent the Marxist position is perhaps most difficult of all. The choice of Miliband is obvious but the choice of Laski and Strachey needs a word of explanation. Both were, at the end of their lives, members of the Labour Party but many of their prolific writings have an explicitly Marxist frame of reference. Hugh Thomas describes Strachey in the 1930s as 'the most articulate spokesman for Marxism in Britain.'[3] Laski's Marxist approach was an important element in his sinister reputation in this country. His standing, however, as a political thinker has been high and international. Because our concern is with delineating the ideological position of a group, not with detailed discussion of the ideas of individuals, the inconsistencies of the last two writers and their many changes of mind and heart are unimportant.

The views of the different groups of thinkers provide so many arguments and counter-arguments that we have not attempted any kind of summary or critique. For the perceptive reader such a conclusion would only be repetitive. What we attempt by way of conclusion is a discussion of the failure of social policy since 1945 to achieve its stated aims. Our conclusion is that the central element in this failure is the nature of capitalism as a set of values and as an economic system, for the ethic of welfare and the ethic of capitalism are in basic opposition. If social policy is to achieve its goals a new ethic is required — social justice — and we outline such a basis.

1

Society, the State, social problems and social policy

Most discussion of the nature of social policy has tended to take place in a theoretical vacuum. Social policy is analysed as if it were an autonomous set of social institutions unconnected with the normal processes of the social and political system in which it is set and which it serves. This lack of theorising is not a politically neutral approach to social policy, as is sometimes claimed, but an implicit conservative stand for it accepts existing social and economic relationships unquestioningly. The thesis in this opening chapter is that it is impossible to understand the nature and functions of social policy without an analysis of the social, economic and political system in which it operates.

Theories of society, of the State, of social problems and of social policy are inter-related. The view a social scientist holds of societal organisation and of the distribution of political and economic power will affect the explanation he gives of the nature of social problems and of the government's response in the form of social policy measures. The link running through the explanations of these phenomena may not always be obvious nor does the relationship always correspond perfectly, but it nevertheless exists to a lesser or greater extent. The compartmentalisation of social science into separate disciplines has helped to obscure this inter-relationship for each specialist discipline tends to be primarily concerned with its own domain with little reference to knowledge beyond its boundaries. This has been particularly true of social administration, partly because of its comparatively late arrival on the scene, and partly because of its heavy concentration on pragmatic, empirical studies of social problems and social policies with little emphasis on social theory. Sociologists, on the other hand, have until recently shied away from studying social problems from a social reform perspective for fear of appearing earnest do-gooders and of tarnishing their newly acquired image of scientific objectivity with the unscientific value judgments which are unavoidable in this area of study.

Any grouping of social theories inevitably over-simplifies the picture and tends to emphasise unity rather than divergence of approach among the various theories involved. On the other hand, however, it has the advantage of highlighting the essential similarities and differences between social theories and their implications. The division of sociological theories of society into order and conflict theories and of political theories of power into pluralist and elitist theories is a simplification of a complex picture, but it enables us to see how sociological theories of society and political theories of power and the State are related, and how they lead to different perspectives on social problems and social policy. All social problems are the product of a process of definition. Social policies are the product of legislation. An understanding of who does the defining, of what is defined as a social problem and how it is defined, as well as of who shapes legislation and in what ways, is clearly crucial to the student of the welfare state.

Order and pluralist theories

The central features of sociological order theories of society[1] are, from the point of view of this discussion, the stress on consensus, stability, integration and functional relations.[2] Every part of society is seen as having a function in the sense that it contributes to the smooth running of the system. Hence, when one part of society is out of line with the others, there is pressure for its re-integration or for some re-alignment of other related parts. In this way, stability in society by and large prevails. It is not only stability based on functional necessity but stability based on consensus of values. Individuals in society, according to this theory, share the same basic social values and are thus agreed on the way they behave towards each other as individuals and as members of groups. Shared values and moral judgments lead to general agreement about modes of behaviour in society. Thus, the value system of society is, according to Parsons, 'the set of normative judgments held by the members of a society who define, with specific reference to their own society, what to them is a good society . . . . With all these qualifications, it is still true to say that values held in common constitute the primary reference point for the analysis of a social system as an empirical system.'[3] This general agreement on social values which leads to agreement on behaviour patterns results in a stable, integrated society which is perpetuated from generation to generation through the two basic social processes of socialisation of the young and of social control for everyone.[4] As Lockwood rather harshly observes in his critique of Parsons, 'the two major threats to a given social system are infants who have not been socialized and individuals who are motivated to deviance or non-conformity.'[5]

Change does not come easily to order theories. Though allowance is made for change, it is seen as an aberration, resulting from dysfunctions within society, from technological changes or from outside pressures. Thus change is an ephemeral phenomenon, perhaps a form of deviance, that is soon overcome so that stability and integration reign again in the social system. There are adequate built-in mechanisms in the social system to absorb the effects of any change and to channel it into harmless processes. It is this claim for almost eternal stability that has provoked Gouldner to declare that 'Parsons has conceived of a social system that is immortal.'[6]

If little allowance is made for change by functionalist theories, conflict is considered almost unthinkable and certainly harmful to society. As Van den Berghe, a sympathetic critic of functionalism, has observed, 'In so far as functionalists have had to take cognizance of problems of conflict and dissension, they have done so in terms of "deviance" or "variance", i.e. an unaccountable aberration from, or modification of, the "dominant pattern" which somehow tends to resolve itself through "institutionalization".'[7] Such a view of social interaction did not seem relevant to the strife ridden cities of American society in the late 1960s. It was difficult to sustain the claim that the urban riots, the Black Power movement, or the mass demonstrations over the war in Vietnam, exemplified consensus on values and interests among the American people. Many critics saw order theories of society as an escape from reality. Such theories tend to see social problems in predominantly non-ideological and non-political ways. As Inkeles has remarked about functionalism, 'Instead of being a lens which sharpens our perspective and puts social reality in focus, it becomes a pair of rose coloured glasses which distort reality, screening out the harsh facts about conflict of purpose and interest in human affairs.'[8]

Parson's view of power in society shows the link between sociological theories of society and political theories of power and the State. He sees power in consensus terms and suggests that it is vested in the government by the public for the fulfilment of collective goals. In his words: 'It is the capacity to mobilize the resources of the society for the attainment of goals for which a general "public" commitment has been made, or may be made. It is mobilization, above all, of the action of persons and groups, which is binding on them by virtue of their position in society.'[9]

3

Perhaps less idealistic than Parsons's views on power are the related pluralist views of political theorists on polititcal power and the functions of the State. Pluralism holds that political power is shared between the State and the various pressure groups in society as well as private individuals. There is no one group in society which dominates and whose interests and ideologies dictate or dominate major government decisions. Concentration of power in one group upsets the equilibrium of society with the result that opposing groups are formed to restore the balance — Galbraith's notion of countervailing power.[10] Here one sees the influence of sociological functionalist views of societal organisation on political views of the distribution of power. If one part of society, i.e. a pressure group, exercises undue influence then the system amoeba-like produces another part — i.e. another pressure group — to counter the excessive influence and thus restore balance and integration. The individual is not lost in the battles between groups and the government because his voice is heard through his membership of groups and through his participation at elections. Moreover, the prevailing consensus on the 'democratic creed', claims Dahl, acts as a check to groups or individuals who may from time to time act in an 'un-American' fashion.[11] Here one sees another important aspect of functionalist consensus theories — their emphasis on consensus of values and the binding force of these values on norms. If the consensus on values and the democratic creed does not suffice, then the government, expressing the will of the people, will intervene to curb the deviant. The State is thus seen as a powerful impartial arbiter of conflicts among groups whenever they arise.

In brief, it is held that in a pluralist society[12]

> there are a number of loci for arriving at political decisions; that business men, trade unions, politicians, consumers, farmers, voters, and many other aggregates all have an impact on policy outcomes; that none of these aggregates is homogeneous for all purposes; that each of them is highly influential over some groups but weak over many others; and that the power to reject undesired alternatives is more common than the power to dominate over outcomes directly.

Fundamental to this view of the role of the State is the belief that there is a common interest in society. Critics of this view point to the obvious inequalities in capitalist industrial societies in terms of income, wealth, political power and social influence and hence to the conflicting interests of groups. In such a society, governments cannot be impartial. Other critics, like Perrow, are disturbed by the natural corollary of pluralist views that 'conflict on the part of the less privileged is automatically deemed disruptive, while the harmony of interests exists for those who have interests worth harmonizing.'[13]

Social problems and social policy

Clearly a view of society that emphasises stability, order, equilibrium, the functional relationship of the various parts of the social system, the pluralistic view of the distribution of power in society and the notion of the impartial State, will tend to see social problems either as problems of deviance or as problems of social disorganisation. The essential difference between the two types of problems is that 'the type of social problem involved in disorganization arises not from people failing to live up to the requirements of their social statuses, as is the case with deviant behaviour, but from the faulty organization of these statuses into a reasonably coherent social system'.[14] The main sources of social disorganisation are 'breakdowns in channels of effective communication between people in a social system', 'defects in the processes of socialisation', and 'faulty arrangements of competing social demands upon people'.[15] Deviant behaviour refers both to nonconformist behaviour and to aberrant behaviour — a distinction between deviant behaviour which is open, unselfish and esteemed by its practitioners and deviant behaviour which is concealed, is for personal gain and is even stigmatised by the deviants themselves. Only aberrant behaviour is considered as causing social problems though it is acknowledged that there is no eternal and definite dividing line between the concepts of aberration and nonconformism.

It is also acknowledged that disorganisation and deviance are related and under certain circumstances they can induce each other. Most social problems are thus seen as the product of the interacting forces of both disorganisation and deviance. Thus, poverty among the population of working age in advanced industrial societies has been divided by Galbraith into insular and case poverty. The first is the result of heavy unemployment in declining regions of the country, i.e. it is the result of social disorganisation. It is the absence of jobs or the inability of declining industries to pay adequate wages that make it impossible for people to fulfil their statuses rather than the failure of the individual to find a job or to work hard. The second is the result of some peculiar characteristic of the individual, i.e. lack of training, low educational standard, excessive procreation, laziness and so on.[16] Not only is some poverty the result of disorganisation and other poverty the result of deviance, but conditions of disorganisation can lead to conditions of deviance with the result that it is not always possible to tell whether a person who is

5

poor is deviant or disorganised.

The disorganisation-deviant view of social problems has dominated social science literature. Many social problems are seen as having little relationship with economic or political inequality and others as having none. Thus their solution is not seen to be directly opposed to vested economic interests in society. Emphasis is placed on 'society' recognising conditions as problematic and hence acting through the government for the solution or amelioration of social problems in a collective, gradual, piecemeal way without disturbing the existing structure of society. No questions are asked about the existing social and economic systems which may be fundamentally connected with the prevalence of social problems. These criticisms will be presented in more detail later on in this chapter.

The strong appeal of the disorganisation-deviant view of social problems, claims Ryan, stems from its ability to appear humane, constructive, and promising without at the same time posing any real threat to the status quo. Using a psychological type of explanation, Ryan argues that a liberal, progressive person faced with the dilemma of having to reconcile inequalities which he condemns in theory with his own privileged position in society resorts to the 'blaming the victim' formula. The liberal progressive 'cannot side with an openly reactionary, repressive position that accepts continued oppression and exploitation as the price of a privileged position for his own class. This is incompatible with his own morality and his basic political principles.'[17] On the other hand, he rejects the solution of radical change on the pretext of its being too extreme while in fact it is because such a change threatens his own privileged position. The result is a compromise solution that is acceptable to the psyche and which leaves the status quo unchanged.[18]

> With such an elegant formulation, the humanitarian can have it both ways. He can, all at the same time, concentrate his charitable interest on the defects of the victim, condemn the vague social and environmental stresses that produced the defect (some time ago), and ignore the continuing effect of victimizing social forces (right now). It is a brilliant ideology for justifying a perverse form of social action designed to change, not society, as one might expect, but rather society's victim.

It is fundamentally the old ideology of 'blaming the victim', claims Ryan, dressed up in modern social scientific jargon.

The broad alliance between functionalism and pluralism which sees social problems in terms of social disorganisation and deviance inevitably considers social policy legislation — i.e. the attempt to deal with social problems — in similar non-political, non-ideological and

non-partisan terms. Though various related interpretations of
social policy flow naturally from this premise, they all see social policy
in mechanistic terms as a functional accompaniment of industrialisation
benefiting all alike. Changes in the industrial system upset the
equilibrium prevailing among the various parts of the social and
economic system with the result that social policy measures become
necessary to restore stability and balance. Industrialisation, for
example, generates geographical mobility and creates strains in
the family system. Hence social policy measures such as old age
pensions or child care legislation become necessary to iron out the
offending strains in the system. Another example would be the
creation of redundancies through the introduction of automated
processes in industry and hence the necessity for social security measures
to re-establish integration in the social system. A slightly different
variation of this approach sees social policy as helping to meet the
general social, economic and manpower needs of the system.
Education measures are introduced to meet the manpower needs of
an expanding industrial system. Emphasis on public provision of
health services becomes imperative in industrial societies for healthy
citizens are a scarce and a precious form of resource. In other words,
the social system has certain needs, it makes certain demands all of
which make social policy measures not only necessary and inevitable but
beneficial to all.

Since social policy measures are seen, according to this approach, as
functionally necessary to economic growth and the stability and
integration of the social system; since no one group dominates in
society and since government is considered the spokesman of the
common weal, there is no insurmountable difficulty in overcoming
opposition — misguided as it is — to social policy whenever it is
encountered. Social policy, as the hand-maiden of technological change
and the adopted child of a consensus society, is characteristic of all
advanced industrial societies. Moreover, this stage in societal evolution,
the welfare state, is seen as one through which all industrially
developing countries will eventually go.[19] The welfare state stage
of societal development is naturally and obviously characterised by a
broad political consensus on ideological issues — by 'the end of
ideology' in Bell's words. In the Western world, Bell asserts, there may
be differences of emphasis and of detail but fundamentally 'there
is today a rough consensus among intellectuals on political issues:
the acceptance of a welfare state; the desirability of decentralized
power; a system of mixed economy and of political pluralism.'[20]
The reason for this is that the main issues and problems have been
resolved and what remains is an assortment of trifling questions
that judicious piecemeal social engineering can settle in a

7

technological society. 'Through industrial development, under democratic auspices', wrote Parsons in aligning himself with Bell, 'the most important legitimately to-be-expected aspirations of the "working class" have in fact been realised.'[21]

In spite of the criticisms levied against functionalist explanations of social policy, they do have the merit of turning attention to the social and economic system and away from such individualistic explanations of social policy as those of Dicey and Hayek. At least they see social policy as emerging out of the processes associated with social and economic change rather than out of the fertile intellect of super-men,[22] or out of a process of mass deception by well-meaning but basically misguided reformers.[23] The two main weaknesses of functionalist explanations of social policy are to be found in their two claims that social policy is 'inevitable' or 'functionally necessary' in its causation and that it is 'neutral' or 'generally beneficial' in its consequences. Goldthorpe referred to the first weakness of functionalist views on social policy in a useful review of attempts to explain social policy. 'A functionalist explanation of the development of social policy requires to be refined and supplemented through analysis which takes an "action" frame of reference; that is analysis in terms of the ends of individuals and groups rather than in terms of the "needs" of society considered as a whole.'[24] Writers on the Left have argued that social policy does not, as a matter of course, benefit equally all those affected. As we shall attempt to show later in this chapter, both the causation and the consequences of social policy are affected by both social class and pressure group conflict and, so far, the pattern and development of social policy have been subordinated to the economic interests of dominant social groups or the ruling class in society.

Conflict and elitist theories

Conflict is a fact of life in modern industrial societies. There can be legitimate discussion about its nature and function but it is difficult to ignore its existence. In Dubin's words,[25]

> Conflict may be labelled dysfunctional or symptomatic of an improperly integrated society. The empirical existence of conflict, however, is not challenged by the stability argument .... The fact of the matter is that group conflict cannot be wished out of existence. It is a reality with which social theorists must deal in constructing their general models of social behaviour.

Conflict theories of society are overshadowed by the Marxist approach in the same way that consensus theories are dominated by the Parsonian approach. It is indeed quite possible, as Coser demonstrates,[26] to accept a consensus model of society which incorporates conflict. In a model of this kind, conflict is seen as having such 'positive functions' as reducing tensions in society, or preventing tensions from building up to violent explosive degrees, making internal changes possible and thus preventing ossification of social structures and so on. Seen in this perspective, social conflict has a cathartic and hence an invigorating effect on the social system. It does not alter the social system itself but it makes changes within the system which render it more effective and spritely.

It is difficult to treat group conflict theories of society of the Coser variety as representing an independent and distinctive perspective on society. Such theories lean either towards the pluralist, pressure group theories we discussed above or towards the Marxist social class conflict theory we shall discuss below. If they see the conflicting groups as possessing more or less equal power and if they hold that conflict can be resolved within the existing socio-economic order, then they are very similar to the pluralist theories. If, on the other hand, they see conflict in society as taking place between groups possessing unequal power and if they maintain that the resolution of conflict over some issues is not possible within the existing political order, then they veer heavily towards the Marxist view. Because of this undecided nature of group conflict theories, discussion on them and on their implications is omitted from this introductory chapter. They are discussed, however, in different parts of chapters 3 and 4. Instead, the discussion in this chapter will be confined to the Marxist conflict models of society because these represent a conceptually different way of looking at society, the State, social problems and social policy.

The Marxist theory of class conflict has more fundamental implications for the social system than theories which restrict themselves to group types of conflict. This is because class conflict centres round the economic relations of society which, the Marxists claim, are the basis of the other types of relationships in society. The economic system forms society's foundation on which the social, political and ideological systems are based. Changes in the economic system bring about changes in the other systems of society. This is not to suggest that all change is due to economic factors or that changes in the economic system cannot be brought about through changes in the other systems of society. Class conflict is seen as natural and inevitable in a stratified society. It is the vehicle of fundamental changes in the whole social system of society. It is basic to the transformation of capitalist societies to socialism. The social system is seen not as a stable integrated structure but as conflict-ridden and always changing. Power is distributed unequally in society with the result that the weaker social groups, though they form the largest section of the population, come to accept, in practice if not in theory, their subordinate position. This is effected through a variety of processes which can only be briefly referred to here.

Coercion, whether open or concealed in institutional social structures, is one such process. Nevertheless, coercion cannot by itself explain the relative stability of modern stratified capitalist societies. One has to look for more subtle forms of social control. One such form of control is the economic dependence of the weak groups of society on the powerful. Another such reason is the legitimation of a set of social values that serves the interests of the powerful groups of society and their transformation into national values that become part of the national cultural heritage. These values are accepted by the weak groups who in this way learn self-control. Thus the general value consensus which prevails is not the result of some objective process through which all members of society have consciously and rationally contributed to the formulation of the value system. On the contrary, as Parkin has argued, 'normative consensus is better understood in terms of the socialisation of one class by another, rather than as independent class agreement or convergence on values.'[27]

Improvements in the material standards of the working class and the provision of social services are other and more positive factors that have contributed to the de-escalation and de-radicalisation of class conflict in society. It is not only the ruled who have changed their outlook but the rulers too have changed in some ways. Marxists admit that today members of the ruling class are not so conspicuous or so arrogant in their attitudes to working class problems as their forefathers were. This, however, does not mean that they have lost their political and economic power as a group. Thus, through coercion, economic dependence, the legitimation of dominant social values, rising economic affluence and welfare state provisions, class conflict in society is reduced and radical change is either contained, slowed down or diluted.

Though Marxists accept that class conflict in modern Britain is less global in scale, less violent in nature and less radical in political intent than it was in the last century for the reasons given above, they do not accept, however, the argument that class conflict has disappeared altogether as is claimed by consensus theorists belonging to the end of ideology or to the managerial revolution groups. As

Birnbaum has noted referring to class conflict, 'The fact that the conflict is often obscured, that it takes partial and particular forms (not involving whole sectors of society pitted consciously against each other but groupings struggling in limited areas), is evidence for a change in the structure of these conflicts and not, as is vulgarly supposed, evidence for their historical elimination.'[28] It is also not true, claim the Marxists, that this consensus is so complete or that it is irreversible so that modern societies are colourless collectivities of 'one-dimensional' men as Marcuse has claimed;[29] there is still enough radicalism in the working class movement of this country, among students and middle class intellectuals, to give hope that progress through political change is still possible, even if at a slow pace.

As in the case of consensus theories, so too with conflict theories the distribution of power in society is crucial. Hence the corresponding political theories of power and of the State stress a pluralistic distribution of political power in consensus theories and an elitist, polarised distribution in the case of conflict theories.[30] Whether one accepts Mills's notion of the 'power elite'[31] or Marx's concept of the 'ruling class' or Bottomore's attempt to synthesise the two,[32] the fundamental argument is that power and wealth in society are concentrated in the hands of a small minority which, in the various ways referred to above, manages to exercise a disproportionate influence on the affairs of a country, thus promoting and perpetuating its own privileged position in society to the detriment of the interests of other groups.

It is acknowledged that the ruling class is made up of sub-groups which vary in number from one country to another and from one period of history to another. Referring to the British situation, Worsley notes that instead of the four elites — the Army, the Church, the politicians and the property owners — which made up the ruling class in the past, today 'there are only two institutional orders, however, within which power is concentrated: the political and the economic order.'[33] This is not to suggest that the other two have disappeared altogether or that they have changed their allegiance, but rather that their importance has faded as a result of the decline of the military strength of the country and the changes that have taken place in the influence of religion in everyday life. The ruling class loses old members and recruits new members over the years through the process of downward and upward social mobility. Nevertheless, it remains a coherent self-perpetuating group. To quote Worsley again, 'The uninterrupted, albeit modified dominance of the property-owning classes in a society which has long been the most highly "proletarianized" in the world, is surely one of the most striking

11

phenomena of modern times.'[34]

Marxist theories of political power hold that governments are either manifestly serving the interests of the ruling class because of their conservative ideology, or in the case of Labour governments, that they are impotent in implementing vigorous anti-capitalist legislation because of the entrenched opposition of Capital and the reigning ideological climate which makes such measures generally unacceptable or even unthinkable. Whereas consensus and pluralist theories tend to identify power with acts of government, conflict and elitist theories tend to see power as resting in other areas of the economic, social and political systems with the result that radical governments, even when they want to, find it difficult to be effective in implementing measures that threaten the status quo. Marxist theorists vary in their estimation of the extent to which radical governments are held back by the ruling class. Birnbaum's opinion on the issue, however, appears to be the one that commands most support. Referring to the situation in a number of European countries, he concludes that property owners and managers have the ability 'if not to impose their will upon the state at least to block or severely limit programs adverse to their interests.'[35] This line of approach by no means claims that no legislative inroads have been made into the privileged terrain of the upper classes but rather that such inroads have been few, and that they have been restricted in scope and depth and that they are often rendered ineffective in practice. The ruling class, it is argued, may have lost odd battles but it has always so far won the war.

Social problems and social policy

Marxist theories give little attention to the sociological processes which generate social problems. They generally rely on the contributions of other conflict theorists who tend to view the main social problems of contemporary industrial societies as being essentially the product of the conflict of economic interests between the two main social classes and between smaller groups in society. In other words, the problem of poverty is regarded neither as the result of cultural deviation by the poor from society's accepted values and norms, nor as the result of social disorganisation, nor as the consequence of some dysfunction in the social system. Rather it is seen as the result of the economic exploitation of one group in society by another. The Marxists see that solving the problem of poverty affects the economic position of the rich and the non-poor in society. They argue too that labelling such potential conflict situations as social problems helps to defuse them for it tends to diffuse responsibility for their existence and continuance and to lead to a search for solutions which do not affect the existing distribution of wealth, income and power. The emphasis is on technical, administrative attempts to solve what are essentially political issues. Rule expresses this argument well when he writes that:[36]

> Race, pollution, poverty, the cities — all of these so-called 'social problems' amount to contests between various groups over the control of desirable resources, including wealth, privilege and, above all, the application of political power. These issues turn on clashes of interest, and thus represent political conflicts. And yet, in the language of the prevailing coalition between government and social science, they are treated instead as social problems, as forms of 'social sickness'. My thesis is that this unwarranted application of clinical language to politics is misleading and dangerous. For it suggests that political conflicts can somehow be resolved a-politically, through the dispassionate intervention of experts instead of through political action. And this suggestion paves the way, in turn, for the imposition of partisan measures in the guise of non-political 'solutions' to 'social problems'.

There is general agreement among social scientists that the definition of a situation as a social problem is related to the power structure of society. Merton, writing from a functionalist point of view, makes this quite clear.[37]

> Social definitions of social problems have this in common with other processes in society: those occupying strategic positions of authority and power of course carry more weight than others in deciding social policy and therefore, among other things, in identifying for the rest what are to be taken as significant departures from social standards. There is not a merely numerical democracy of judgement in which every man's approval is assigned the same voting power in defining a condition as a social problem.

Merton, however, does not make clear the relationship between power and social class. If power is concentrated in the hands of the ruling class, as the Marxists maintain, then the definition of what officially constitutes a social problem, particularly one that is essentially a conflict of economic interests between social classes, will be the domain of the ruling class and its allies. There may, of course, be other definitions of the same problem but for social policy measures it is

13

the ruling class definition that counts. There may also be situations where economic interests are not directly involved and where the conflict of definitions is between groups other than social classes. Nevertheless, social class is a determinant of what is defined as a social problem in the crucial areas. Ross and Staines refer to this relationship between social class and social problems as follows:[38]

> Despite the creation of many status gradations in a complex technological environment, economic class still provides some of the most obvious examples of the linkage between group membership and problem perception. Thus we expect, and find, a business view of the problem of unemployment and a labor view; a business view of the problem of inflation and a labor view.

It is significant that the examples cited by Ross and Staines are situations with strong and direct conflict of economic interests between the classes. Not all situations defined as social problems, however, are of this nature. There are many where conflict of economic interests is neither strong nor clear and others where it exists in a mild form. It is possible to consider social problems within a theoretical framework that adopts a continuum of social problems ranging from those which are primarily conflicts of moral values to those which are primarily conflicts of economic interests. These are ideal types and, though all social problems will involve conflicts of both moral values and economic interests, some will be more easily placed at one end of the continuum than the other. Other problems will belong to the middle part of the continuum and for some others there will be disagreement as to their proper classification.

Conflict and consensus theories differ in another important respect in the way they view social problems. Consensus theories of society tend to consider behaviour which departs from conventional standards as problematic, for not only do they assume a uniformity in the values and norms of society but they also consider that such behaviour as is generally accepted is best. Conflict theories of society, on the other hand, accept greater cultural diversity in society and they tend to question the legitimacy of generally accepted forms of behaviour. Horton, in a concise discussion of order and conflict theories of social problems, expresses this difference of approach well: 'The conflict theorist invariably questions the legitimacy of existing practices and values; the order theorist accepts them as the standard of health.'[39] Hence, forms of behaviour, which from a consensus point of view are considered as social problems of morality, may from a conflict point of view be accepted as simply another form of behaviour with no implications for public policy. Indeed, some of these different forms of behaviour may even be seen in positive terms as spearheading change in the traditional forms of conduct which the conflict theorist does not wholly accept.

Seen from a conflict perspective, concern for social problems is tantamount to concern about the social system itself. A conflict approach to social problems is much less comfortable than an order approach for it seeks changes not only within the existing system but of parts of the system itself. The study of social problems is, as Sykes has written, 'nothing less than the study of what is considered the satisfactory and unsatisfactory organization of society, not in terms of minor concerns arousing momentary public indignation but in terms of the major elements of the social structure'.[40] Seen from a Marxist point of view, the resolution of social problems can only be achieved with the change of the entire capitalist system.

As we shall see in chapter 5, Marxists do not dismiss the benefits of the welfare state to the working class. They do insist, however, that the welfare state cannot advance beyond certain limits without meeting implacable resistance from the ruling class. Whether the welfare state can proceed beyond this critical point through parliamentary means depends on various factors discussed in chapters 5 and 6. Marxists thus view social policy as resulting primarily from the on-going process of class conflict in society. They do not discount other forces but they hold that class conflict is the central generating force behind social policy. Industrialisation is a contributory factor in the sense that it creates a working class conscious of its power and prepared to back up its demands for improvements in its living conditions through political and industrial action. The response of the ruling class to these demands will vary from country to country, according to the relative strength of the working class, the cultural tradition of the country and the ability of the leadership of the ruling class to see that such demands, if properly handled, can be as much benefit to itself as to the working class. The fact that there are rare examples of such policy measures being introduced without any apparent pressure from the working class does not invalidate this thesis, for there are always exceptions to every rule, and because the potentiality of class struggle as well as the actual conflict can exert pressure. The potentiality of class conflict as a motivating force for social reform is crucial to the Marxist thesis. It explains bursts of social policy legislation, such as the one after the last war, when class conflict is not apparently strong. It is generally agreed that social policy measures introduced at the end of the last war had been discussed during the war as a spur to winning the war. It is also agreed, however, that without such social policy measures the political and industrial unrest of the 1920s could well have repeated itself. That the mood of the general public was eager for changes in the social and economic structure of the country was shown by the landslide victory of the Labour Party in 1945. The fact that the reforms introduced by the Labour Party did little to change the basic economic structure of British society is seen by Marxists as proof of the thesis that even reforming governments find it difficult to undermine the position of the ruling class for the reasons discussed earlier in this chapter.

Social problems and social policy — an assessment

In this last section we set out the theoretical framework within which we seek to analyse social problems and social policy. We adopt a conflict approach, for both social problems and social policy reflect events and processes in society and we see society as essentially conflict-ridden. In the last analysis, social problems are primarily the product of social conflicts involving the economic interests and the value systems of competing population groups and social classes. At one end of the continuum are those social problems which are the product primarily of conflicts of economic interests. It makes little sense, for example, to consider poverty and unemployment as deviations from the social norm as has been the traditional functionalist view. They are more realistically seen as conflicts between the poor and the wealthy, the unemployed and employers respectively.

At the other end of the continuum are those problems which are produced primarily by conflicts between the value systems of the particular group concerned and of the rest of society. Homosexuality, for example, is a social problem in the sense that the value system and the behaviour of homosexuals is in conflict with the moral value system and the behaviour of the heterosexual majority. Abortion involves conflict of moral values and behaviour between those who accept abortion and those who do not. At this same end of the continuum is another group of social problems which are the result of some physical or mental malfunctioning which challenges the ethical value system of society — deafness, blindness, mental handicap and so on. They are the product not of conflicts between the value system of the particular group and the rest of society but rather of conflict between the problematic situation of the group in question and society's ethical value system. The inability of such groups to live a normal life without help and the ability of their fellow citizens, if they so wish, to 'normalise' their lives, makes their situation challenging to certain ethical values.

16

Many social problems will be plotted in the middle of the continuum for they involve conflicts of economic interests and value systems fairly equally. Stealing involves a conflict of economic interests between those who own goods and those who steal them. Though this can and does involve all sections of society, it is primarily a conflict between property owners and a section of the rest of society. Stealing, however, involves more than conflict of economic interests between the relevant groups. It also involves a conflict between the value systems of those who consider stealing as morally wrong in principle and those who do not or are able to justify it to themselves in certain circumstances.

Looking at social problems as forms of social conflict has important implications for their solutions. It highlights the political nature of problems of the first category and it indicates that their solution must mean the improvement of the living conditions of one group in society at the expense of another. It is not possible, for example, to abolish relative poverty without affecting the living standards of the non-poor. Relative poverty is very near to income inequality and the reduction, let alone abolition, of income inequality means that some groups will benefit and others will lose. The value of this approach to social problems of this kind is that it forces policy makers to face stark realities. It is a move away from what might be called the 'technocratic' approach to social problems which has dominated social policy so far. This approach assumes that if only we knew more about the causation of such problems and if there were the necessary resources, then these problems would be solved. Knowledge, staff and adequate finance may be necessary but in themselves they do not provide the solution to such problems. To see the eradication of social problems as depending on a range of piecemeal welfare programmes is to cherish a comfortable illusion. It is to pursue what Parenti refers to as 'the VISTA approach to economic maladies; a haphazard variety of public programs are initiated, focussing on the poor and ignoring the system of power, privilege and profit which makes them poor. It is a little like blaming the corpse for the murder.'[41]

The approach to social problems which we suggest also recognises the existence of conflicting value systems and forms of behaviour without necessarily apportioning blame and moral worthlessness. It is a more open and realistic approach to problems involving conflict of value systems and it may perhaps lead to a more understanding attitude towards groups whose value systems and behaviour are different from those of the majority in society. It goes without saying, however, that even in a socially just and egalitarian society where economic domination and exploitation will either cease or be substantially reduced, there will still be problems of value conflict. No society can accept all forms of value systems and behaviour. Social problems of this type are part and parcel of life in society.

If social problems are the product of conflict, then attempts to solve them are primarily attempts to reconcile conflicting economic interests and value systems. A conflict situation is by nature problematic and unstable and begs for redefinition. It may well be that the 'solution' is often no more than a compromise with the result that the conflict situation remains. This, however, does not invalidate the thesis that it is the forces inherent in the conflict situation that are the driving impulse for change and for the redefinition of the situation. As Rex has pointed out, the resultant redefinitions are initially truce situations which eventually may either become permanent features of society or be redefined into new truce situations.[42] Conflict and change are on-going natural processes in society. Social policy is thus primarily the result of the constant attempts of various groups in society to improve or redefine their situation vis-à-vis that of other groups.

It is important for our discussion to distinguish between the two stages of social policy formulation. The first stage of conflict decides whether legislative change will take place, while the second decides the actual form and shape of legislation. There is clearly an overlap between these two stages as well as between the groups involved in the conflicts during these stages. Nevertheless, it is useful to distinguish between them for it enables us to conceptualise more clearly the processes of social policy formulation. As a rule, the forces and groups involved in the first stage are of a broader and higher level than those involved in the second stage. One can, for example, distinguish between the forces that led to the decision by the government to broaden its involvement in the provision of elementary education and the pressures that determined the actual shape and scope of the Education Act, 1870.

The second stage of social policy formulation is primarily one of pressure group 'pecking' activity. The various groups whose economic interests and value systems are affected join in the conflict in an attempt to shape legislation in accordance with their views or to their advantage. It is not a haphazard form of infighting; rather there is a 'pecking order' that favours the powerful pressure groups. This analysis of the second stage of social policy formulation applies to all types of social problems.

The first stage of social policy formulation is much more difficult to analyse than the second. It is important to state clearly that the type of explanation of social policy formulation at the first stage varies according to whether the social problem concerned is primarily one of conflicting economic interests or social values. In the case of problems involving conflict of economic interests, social class interests and hence social class conflict is the primary force. This follows from our acceptance of the thesis that in a society where the means of production are in private hands and where the profit motive for private ends dominates the operation of the means of production, there is an inherent conflict of economic interests between the two main social classes — the working class and the upper class. The form and intensity of class conflicts obviously change over the years but they do not disappear altogether in a capitalist society. This conflict can be both actual and potential in the sense that if certain improvements are not made in the standards of living of the working class, conflict is likely to follow. Working class pressure on governments and on the upper class also takes various forms ranging from the right to vote, strikes of different types, wider, peaceful political activity and violent political agitation. Thus, when we assert that social policy formulation in issues involving primarily conflict of economic interests is the result of social class conflict, we do not mean open and violent strife between the two major classes. We mean various forms of actual or potential pressure are exerted by the working class and its allies to redefine certain situations.

It is in this sense that one can maintain that this area of social policy largely consists of a series of concessions won by or granted to the working class. Like most concessions, they are compromises in the sense that they do not constitute a victory for either side. Only a detailed examination of each social policy measure can show whether the compromise favours the working class or the upper class.

The second stage of social policy formation referred to earlier is crucial in this. The decision of the Liberal government in 1911, for example, to legislate for some form of income security in illness and unemployment was the result of both actual and potential class conflict. The use of the insurance principle, however, the level of benefits, and the multitude of other constituent parts of the National Insurance Act, 1911, were the result of the conflicts and bargains between the various pressure groups involved. Since working class pressure groups were neither so strong nor so proficient in the art of exerting pressure as the other groups involved, and since the whole confrontation was taking place within an ideological climate that favoured the upper classes, the framing of the 1911 Act was favourable to upper class interests. The second stage of social policy formation acts as a check to the victories of the working class. When one also bears in mind that the actual implementation of social policy legislation generally falls short of its stated intentions, the limited effects of social policy provision on the stratified nature of society becomes clear. The distribution of economic and political power in society is such that if social policy is to improve, even slightly, the conditions of the working class, it must adopt a policy of over-kill.

The social class conflict explanation of social policy does not apply to those aspects of social policy which are concerned either with clear issues of morality or with issues that have no obvious economic implications. Legislation concerned with capital punishment, homosexuality, divorce and abortion comes within this category. Here one can attribute social policy measures either to the efforts of philanthropy, to private individuals, or to pressure group activity of a specialised non-party political nature. Such efforts are sometimes in line with public opinion (or what is thought to be public opinion) and sometimes not. The essential point for this discussion is that though they involve conflict between those demanding and those resisting change, it is conflict which cannot be considered as being of a social class nature. Reforms involving issues of this nature may gain less support among the working class than among the middle and upper classes for such reforms usually follow or accompany changes in the dominant social values — changes which originate in the middle and upper classes and then spread downwards in society to the working class. There is, so to speak, a social value lag which accounts for the apparently reactionary response of the working class to some such social policy measures. It is a corollary of the thesis that the values of the dominant class are the reigning values in society and that the definition of social problems owes more to the values of this class than to the larger but less powerful class of working people.

Our analysis of social policy formulation may not fit each and every piece of legislation. Ideologically, it is an attempt to move away from the early functionalist and from the strong humanitarian explanations of social policy development. Ideologically and theoretically it is also a departure from loose pluralist explanations which merely attribute the development of social policy to a variety of factors without any attempt either to give a relative weight to these factors or to relate them to any sociological theory of society.

In this chapter, we have outlined the relationship between sociological theories of society and political theories of power on one hand, and explanations of social problems and social policy on the other. We continue this discussion in chapters 2 — 5 where we analyse the views of selected writers on the nature and functions of the welfare state and in chapter 6 where we discuss in some detail our understanding of the welfare state within the general framework of social justice.

2

THE ANTI-COllECTiViSTS

The last hundred years have seen a vast expansion of government
activity in all spheres of life but particularly in what may be loosely
called the social aspects. It is only in the last thirty years or so that this
expansion has spread in a large way to the economic sector of the
nation's life. This general trend, which gained momentum in the last
quarter of the nineteenth century and whose force has not yet been
expended, may be seen as inaugurating the age of collectivism. It has
been a movement that has alarmed many and satisfied others. Its
fundamental principle, noted Dicey – one of its earliest and most
vigorous critics – 'is faith in the benefit to be derived by the mass
of the people from the action or intervention of the State even in
matters which might be, and often are, left to the uncontrolled
management of the persons concerned'.[1] Critics of collectivism have
varied both in their vehemence towards the movement and in their
faith in the philosophy of individualism that has inspired all such
criticism. Anti-collectivism, like collectivism, cannot be compounded
into one mould. In this chapter, we discuss the strongest brand of
anti-collectivism – the views of Hayek, Friedman and Powell. These
three writers stand for a form of social organisation that was known
as liberalism in the nineteenth century. If we have refrained from calling
them liberals – as perhaps some of them would have preferred – it is
not for any wish to represent their views as negative but because
liberalism today stands for such a wide spectrum of political ideology
that it has lost all meaning. The term liberalism confuses rather than
clarifies discussion today.

Social values

Views on the welfare state — both favourable and unfavourable —
represent a fusion of scientific evidence and of ideology. It is more
than likely that, on fundamental issues of welfare provision, ideology
plays a more important part than scientific evidence, for on such
issues there can be little true evidence. It is difficult to see, for
example, what true scientific evidence could be provided either
in favour of or against State provision of retirement pensions for
the elderly in industrial societies, since all such societies provide such
benefits. Scientific evidence, however, may play a more important
role than ideology on secondary and administrative issues, i.e.
whether retirement pensions should be increased annually, whether
they should include special additions for heating during the winter
months and so on. The social values that people hold can affect not
only their decisions on welfare provision but they can also colour
their interpretation of scientific evidence. It is for this reason that
special attention is being given in this and the subsequent three
chapters to the social values of critics of the welfare state. As will
become clear, the different groups of these critics differ not only in
what social values they hold but also in the extent to which they
support the same values.

Freedom or liberty, individualism and inequality are the
fundamental social values of anti-collectivists. Often freedom and
individualism are used interchangeably by them and though there is
a close affinity and overlap between these two values, they are
nevertheless different in several important perspectives. Liberty
or freedom is seen primarily in negative terms as the absence of
coercion. Liberty, writes Hayek, is 'that condition of men in which
coercion of some by others is reduced as much as possible in society'.[2]
The central idea in this conception of liberty is the lack of coercion of
one individual by another. Coercion occurs 'when one man's actions
are made to serve another man's will, not for his own but for the
other's purpose'.[3] In this way, the coerced person becomes a mere
tool in the achievement of the ends of the oppressor. As a result, he
tends to lose his identity 'as a thinking and valuing person'.[4] Yet
if coercion is to be avoided, there must be known sanctions against
those who attempt it. In other words, coercion can only be avoided
by the threat of coercion. Hayek acknowledges this and postulates
that the State has been freely entrusted by all the citizens with the
duty of enforcing such sanctions against those who violate certain
known rules. He sees this institutionalisation of coercion as freely
acceded to by all and as benefiting all equally in spite of the
stratified nature of society and the concentration of power in certain

population groups. Once these rules of non-interference have been established, the State acts as the protector of the interests of all; it ensures that they pursue their interests unmolested by others. Coercion by the State, though necessary in a few pre-defined areas, becomes an instrument for liberty. In this way, liberty becomes in a sense a positive concept because though it does not offer us any rewards, it 'leaves it to us to decide what use we shall make of the circumstances in which we find ourselves'.[5]

Liberty is valued both as an end in itself and as a means to an end. It is the natural right of all men and social organisation must safeguard it unless certain proven circumstances exist to justify its curtailment. Liberty is also an instrumental value for the promotion of knowledge, progress and other desirable conditions in society. It may well be that only a minute minority of individuals use their freedom to promote social improvement or to add to human knowledge but then innovation has always been the result of the activities of a few individuals. Thus liberty is not a terminal and an instrumental value in abstract terms only but it is also to the benefit of both the individual and of society in general. All in all, 'Freedom is a rare and delicate plant'[6] writes Friedman, echoing the views of other anti-collectivists. Hence, any government measures that promote other social values and which may affect liberty are deprecated. As a result, there is unanimous agreement among anti-collectivists that one cannot support both liberty and substantive equality, for example, for in the last analysis one cannot be both for and against substantial government intervention, on the assumption that there is no likelihood of the rich sharing their wealth with the rest voluntarily. There are, of course, other reasons why anti-collectivists are against material equality, and these we shall discuss later in this chapter.

If the individual is free from all coercion by other individuals and from unwarranted coercion by the State, then he will respond by exerting himself to the utmost limit of his abilities to the advantage of himself and his country. Individualism is complementary to freedom and one cannot exist without the other. Non-intervention by the State promotes individualism and vice versa a strong sense of individualism makes unnecessary or impossible large scale State intervention or coercion. But what is individualism? In its grandiose conception, individualism is a 'theory of society, an attempt to understand the forces which determine the social life of man'.[7] In this statement, Hayek attempts 'to refute the silliest of the common misunderstandings: the belief that individualism postulates (or bases its arguments on the assumption of) the existence of isolated or self-contained individuals'.[8] Individuals are not self-contained entities but rather they are irrational, fallible beings who pursue their interests in relation to other human beings. Social phenomena can, therefore, be satisfactorily understood only 'through our understanding of individual actions, directed toward other people and guided by their expected behaviour'.[9] They cannot be understood, as some sociological theories maintain, by considering society or other such social wholes 'as entities sui generis which exist independently of the individuals which compose them'.[10] Individualism is in brief an atomistic theory of social organisation.

On a less exalted plane, individualism constitutes 'a set of political maxims'[11] derived from a particular view of the State. What are these political maxims? Individualism prefers to view man 'not as a highly rational and intelligent but as a very irrational and fallible being, whose individual errors are corrected only in the course of a social process'.[12] For this reason no one man can have a panoramic view of society and can know what ought or ought not to be done on a grand scale. Rather, through their interaction, by correcting, modifying or adding to what others have done, individuals produce achievements that are beyond their individual capacities. This 'spontaneous collaboration of free men often creates things which are greater than their individual minds can ever fully comprehend'.[13] It follows from this that if men are allowed to strive for what they themselves consider desirable, nothing but good will result. The spontaneous network of individual checks and counterchecks is enough to eliminate excessive demands, unworkable plans and so on by particular individuals. Any serious interference with this process by the State is bound to produce more harm than good. Competition even by imperfect and irrational men is the ideal road to progress.

Individualism is not against organisations or associations of men striving for a common goal. In fact, voluntary associations are an integral part of individualism. What individualism is opposed to is the use of coercion to bring about such associations. Indeed, individualism attributes to voluntary associations and voluntary institutions a very large role in social organisation. The family, the school, the church and so on are just as important as the State. In fact, 'much for which the coercive action of the State is usually invoked can be done better by voluntary collaboration.'[14]

Individualism is not a ticket for nonconformity. By stressing voluntary collaboration between individuals and by exalting the virtues of social institutions, individualism does not open the floodgates to libertarianism. In fact, the opposite is the case. By postulating that the individual is an imperfect human being, individualism asks for humility and conformity. Thus, Hayek argues that 'the individual, in participating in the social processes, must be ready and willing to adjust himself to changes and to submit to conventions which are not the result of intelligent design, whose justification in the particular instance may not be recognizable and which to him will often appear unintelligible and irrational.'[15] Thus, individualism tapers off into conservatism. On the one hand it exalts individual drive and initiative and on the other it urges conformity to existing norms.

Individualism is a composite creed with contradictory strands but with one theme dominating – man must be as free as possible to pursue his interests and to bear the consequences of his actions. It is this kind of individualism that has created Western European civilisation, that led to the economic prosperity of the nineteenth and early twentieth centuries and which, anti-collectivists argue, is threatened by the egalitarian policies of the welfare state today. Material equality and freedom are seen as antithetical and, as Friedman has declared, 'one cannot be both an egalitarian . . . and a liberal.'[16] Equality of incomes from work is seen as undesirable economically because of its feared deleterious effects on work incentives and because of the abolition of social esteem attached to different occupations which acts as a guide for recruiting people to those occupations. Equality is also politically unacceptable, since to be achieved – bearing in mind people's unwillingness to give up privileges voluntarily – it would involve government coercion. Even if equality had no injurious effects on the economy, anti-collectivists would reject equality for they would rather, or so they claim, be free to be poor rather than be coerced by the State into relative affluence. Even inheritance of wealth that leads to inequality is justified, both on grounds of the freedom of the individual to dispose of his wealth as he pleases and on utilitarian grounds: abolition of wealth inheritance would lead to nepotism – parents placing their children in positions of authority to assure a comfortable living for them – which 'would cause a waste of resources and an injustice much greater than is caused by the inheritance of property'.[17] Thus, the anti-collectivists support equality of freedom and inequality of incomes. It is not a contradictory statement because it is feared that in order to achieve equality of incomes, one would have to sacrifice equality of freedom, which is the reigning social value for the anti-collectivists. Hayek reflects the general consensus: 'Equality of the general rules of law and conduct . . . is the only kind of equality conducive to liberty and the only equality which we can secure without destroying liberty. Not only has liberty nothing to do with any other sort of equality, but it is even bound to produce inequality in many respects.'[18] Inequality of income and wealth has been so far the only compatible accompaniment of freedom and individualism and it is likely to remain so.

Societal organisation

Anti-collectivists devote little time to the sociological discussion on
the stratified nature of modern industrial societies. They obviously
accept the existence of income and wealth inequality but they do
not consider the degree of inequality either excessive or harmful to
society. On the contrary, the extent of inequality is both justified and
conducive to economic growth, bearing in mind that men are what they
are and that their contribution to the general welfare of society varies.
Capitalism has reduced excessive inequality to the present appropriate
level. Capitalism, states Friedman, 'leads to less inequality than
alternative systems of organisation and . . . the development of
capitalism has greatly lessened the extent of inequality.'[19] Contrasts
between rich and poor in terms of income and general standard of
living have been reduced. Hayek welcomes this trend and regards 'the
degree of social equality that the United States has achieved as wholly
admirable'.[20]

Market forces such as competition, supply and demand, profit, free
wage bargaining and so on have played a large part in this general
rise of social equality. These same forces are also the guarantors of
individual freedom because they ensure that no one group in society
controls both economic and political power. Unlike the situation in
centrally planned societies where these two forms of power are
vested in the government, in democracies not only are they separated
but they are also dispersed among a multitude of groups and
individuals. 'By removing the organisation of economic activity',
maintains Friedman, 'from the control of political authority, the
market eliminates this source of coercive power. It enables economic
strength to be a check to political power, rather than a reinforcement.'[21]

Monopolies of both business and labour are deprecated for they
limit competition and voluntary transactions. The growth of large
trade unions and enterprises may have slightly reduced free
competition but it has not created a state of monopoly. 'The most
important fact about enterprise monopoly', writes Friedman, 'is its
relative unimportance from the point of view of the economy as a
whole.'[22] There are thousands of businesses, millions of self-employed
men in the United States so that one cannot talk of monopoly
business. The same situation applies to trade unions, though
anti-collectivists detect unhealthy signs in this field. Government
policy towards trade unions has been far more permissive than
towards private enterprise. The result has been that trade unions
'have become the only important instance in which governments
signally fail in their prime function — the prevention of coercion and
violence'.[23] Trade union powers in respect of picketing and the closed

shop are particularly singled out for criticism. Such powers give trade unions coercive powers over workers, industrialists, consumers, the public at large and even the government. In the more fiery language of Powell, trade union officials can 'tyrannise' all and sundry. If such behaviour were exhibited by businessmen, it would have been deemed unlawful and hence coerced by the State. In this way, anti-collectivists see power concentrated, if anywhere, in the hands of trade unions, rather than of employers as the Marxists would argue. This concentration of power in trade unions is not only politically suspect but it is also deemed to be economically detrimental for it reduces the free interplay of market forces that is so necessary for economic growth.

Governments can be impartial and independent and they often are. Nevertheless, they are also influenced by pressure groups and vested interests from all directions. This is particularly true of Labour governments, according to Powell, which believe in centrally conceived national planning. He ridicules the general belief in the omnipotence of governments and declares: 'Lift the curtain and "the state" reveals itself as a little group of fallible men in Whitehall, making guesses about the future, influenced by political pressures and partisan prejudices . . .'[24] As we shall show in the following section, anti-collectivists have more clearly formulated ideas of what the role of government should be than of the way in which it actually operates today.

The role of governments

The anti-collectivists' dislike of collectivism is partly ideological and partly pragmatic. It is based on a four-fold assertion, some of it reminiscent of nineteenth-century liberalism and some of it of a more contemporary nature. It is feared that substantial government intervention is socially disruptive, it is wasteful of resources, it promotes economic inefficiency and it obliterates individual freedom.

The welfare state promotes disruption of the social fabric by recognising that people have social rights. The 'translation of a want or need into a right is one of the most widespread and dangerous of modern heresies',[25] writes Powell. It is dangerous because not only does it provide 'unlimited fuel for dissatisfaction, it provides unlimited scope for the fostering of animosities between one section of potential recipients and another'.[26] An individual who has come to believe that he has a social right must feel that the State or the community must provide him with the service or goods in question and that, where it fails, it can and must be forced to do so. The result is that minorities feel aggrieved and justified in using force to obtain what they feel are their rights. Squatters, gypsies, social security beneficiaries, students and so on have come to cultivate the technique of violence as a method to achieve their aims. This has reached terrible proportions with the result that the great silent majority of peaceful citizens 'groan under the tyranny of small minorities' to use Powell's graphic phrase. The State and social reformers are to blame for this state of affairs which has become a vicious circle. 'Politics is thus caught in a vicious circle. Violence feeds on "social grievances" which derive from unfulfillable "rights". The result is that ever wider and deeper State intervention is demanded while the State has itself become the source, as well as the focus, of social grievances.'[27] The only way out of the vicious circle is the renunciation of the concept of social rights and the wholesale dismantling of the welfare state apparatus.

The criticism of resource waste is based on two assumptions that are taken more or less as self-evident by the anti-collectivists. The first is that 'at nil price demand is infinite',[28] whereas supply is limited in the social services. By providing services free of charge, governments stimulate false demand. This is wasteful enough in itself but the situation becomes even worse when the service cannot meet the entire demand due to insufficient resources. The providers of a service find it impossible to sort out justifiable from unjustifiable demand with the consequent misallocation of services. Even when the providers of the service manage to differentiate between genuine and false demand, they have had to use up precious time in the process. The second assumption is that social services which are funded and administered by the central government breed a spirit of alienation and they engender 'a continual deafening chorus of complaint'.[29] This spirit of alienation involves lack of pride in the service, perpetual demand for more expenditure, neglect of other possible sources of improvement and a tendency to denigrate the service. 'The universal Exchequer financing of the service', wrote Powell reflecting his experience of running the National Health Service, 'endows everyone providing as well as using it with a vested interest in denigrating it, so that it presents what must be the unique spectacle of an undertaking that is run down by everyone engaged in it.'[30] Both the users and the providers of the service lose all sense of proportion in their demands for more resources and they tend to blame individuals and personalities for lack of unlimited resources, rather than recognise the real restrictions imposed by economic considerations. Thus, freely provided social services have an in-built mechanism for increased wastefulness and an ever-growing sense of alienation among users and providers.

The third major criticism of collectivism is that it is inefficient

from the economic point of view. Anti-collectivists base their
argument on the fundamental assumption that the price and profit
mechanism of the private market is the most efficient guarantor
of economic growth. Government monopoly of a service is inefficient
because it leads to unnecessary expenditure because of lack of proper
concern about costs and efficiency. Criticising government intervention
in industrial training, Powell argues that it inevitably led to rocketing
expenditure. 'Freed from its anchorage in profit and loss, it was
predictable that training would rise like a balloon and float into the
stratosphere.'[31] Government monopoly is also undesirable because
it kills off competition and experimentation, both of which are
necessary for economic growth.[32] Competition means more economical
use of resources and experimentation leads to new forms of production
and distribution. Government monopoly is also undesirable for it
locates all the planning decisions in one government agency, rather
than allowing them to be shared by a number of private agencies. In
major issues, it is not clear which is the right course of action and hence
by locating decisions in one government agency, there is the risk   of
wrong decisions affecting millions of people. This is not the case for
private agencies, where different decisions may be taken on the same
issue thus providing safeguards against massive errors.[33] Not only
has knowledge on issues involving planning on a large scale been
inadequate so far, but it will always remain so because of the
complexity of the quantitative and qualitative attributes of such
planning. Only collectivists suffering from 'synoptic delusion' can
dispute this, claims Hayek.[34] Powell sums up the discussion on the
inability of governments to plan on a national scale in a way other
anti-collectivists would accept. Discussing the idea of any government
national plan, he argues that 'we can assert three things with
confidence: it is likely to be wrong, dead wrong, in its major
assumptions: its errors will do the maximum damage because they
will be imposed on the whole of the economy and they will be persisted
in long after they have been revealed, because governments are the
slowest of all creatures to admit themselves mistaken and a State
plan is, of all plans, the most inflexible.'[35]

The fourth and final major criticism of collectivism is that it leads
to tyranny and dictatorship because it inevitably extirpates individual
freedom. National planning in a democracy is difficult not only
because of inadequate data but also because there is no unanimity in
values as to what is desirable and legitimate. Collective planning,
therefore, has to be imposed from above in situations of lack of general
consensus. In Hayek's words, 'planning leads to dictatorship because
dictatorship is the most effective instrument of coercion and the
enforcement of ideals, and as such essential if central planning on a

large scale is to be possible.'[36] This totalitarianism may take various political forms, including fascism, socialism and communism.

Large-scale State planning also leads to dictatorship in another way indicated earlier in this chapter. In a democracy, argues Friedman, political and economic power are separated while in socialist societies they are concentrated in the hands of the government. He sees this relationship between the two forms of power as the crucial determining factor of any society. 'There is an intimate connection', he writes, 'between economics and politics, that only certain combinations of political and economic arrangements are possible and that, in particular, a society which is socialist cannot also be democratic in the sense of guaranteeing individual freedom.'[37] This does not mean that economic freedom necessarily means political freedom as well. It does mean, however, that without economic freedom there cannot be political freedom. If 'economic power is joined to political power, concentration seems almost inevitable. On the other hand, if economic power is kept in separate hands from political power, it can serve as a check and a counter to political power.'[38] Hayek voiced very similar sentiments when he pointed out that 'economic planning would involve direction of almost the whole of our life. There is hardly an aspect of it, from our primary needs to our relations with our family and friends, from the nature of our work to the use of our leisure over which the planner would not exercise his "conscious control".'[39]

As was mentioned earlier in this chapter, anti-collectivists are against enterprise monopolies. Though State and private monopolies may have certain common disadvantages, they are fundamentally different. State monopoly is different from private monopoly, according to Powell, because 'we know that the State already has extensive powers to counteract monopoly where it is against the public interest and that even if it did not have enough, it could be given still more. We know too that the State's judgment of the public interest is clearer and its action in the public interest firmer when it is not itself a party to the issue; when it has not its own chickens to protect and cherish.'[40]

In spite of their insistence that government intervention is fatal to economic growth and liberty, the anti-collectivists are not against all government intervention. 'The consistent liberal', writes Friedman, 'is not an anarchist.'[41] What rules, what guidelines are there, however, to distinguish acceptable from unacceptable State intervention? What is the appropriate role of government in societal affairs?

Friedman's discussion is the clearest exposition of this issue. He considers three areas which 'cannot be handled through the market at all, or can be handled at so great a cost that the use of political

channels may be preferable'.[42] The first such role of government is to
act as 'rule-maker and umpire'. In discussion, however, he seems to
belittle the role of the State as a rule-maker and to attribute most of
the rules that govern conditions among citizens to 'the unintended
outcome of custom, accepted unthinkingly'.[43] In his summary, too,
he ignores the rule-making role of the State. He writes: 'These then
are the basic roles of government in a free society: to provide a
means whereby we can modify the rules, to mediate differences among
us on the meaning of rules and to enforce compliance with the rules
on the part of those few who would otherwise not play the game.'[44]
Governments acting in the capacity of umpires will tend mainly to
maintain the status quo which, as far as the anti-collectivists are
concerned, is an adherence to the traditional limited interventionist
role of government. The State can exercise its limited role as umpire
in a number of fields. A competitive market system, for example,
needs legal backing in order to operate efficiently. Hayek makes this
point: 'An effective competitive system needs an intelligently
designed and continuously adjusted legal framework as much as any
other.'[45] Another obvious area of State umpiring is the administration
of justice which Powell maintains has been neglected by successive
governments in contemporary Britain. 'The State in Britain today',
he declares, 'is in desperate danger of neglecting and starving its own
unique and essential business in order to thrust its arms up to the
sockets into business which does not need it and fares better
without.'[46]

The second appropriate area of government intervention, as
suggested by Friedman, relates to 'cases in which strictly voluntary
exchange is either exceedingly costly or practically impossible.
There are two general classes of such cases: monopoly and similar
market imperfections and neighbourhood effects.'[47] Though against
monopolies in principle (particularly government monopolies),
Friedman concedes that a monopoly may be necessary for reasons
of technical efficiency and that in exceptional cases such monopoly
may be entrusted to the government. Cases of technical monopoly,
however, are very few and they change over time. They relate to
'a service or commodity that is regarded as essential' and where
'its monopoly power is sizable';[48] perhaps services like telephones
and the post office.

Government intervention on grounds of 'neighbourhood effects'
arises 'when actions of individuals have effect on other individuals for
which it is not feasible to charge or recompense them'.[49] This is a
difficult area and it can be interpreted both widely and narrowly
depending on one's general attitude towards the desirability of
government action. Thus Friedman argues that the provision of

31

free city parks by the government may be justified but not the
provision of national parks for this reason:[50]

> For the city park, it is extremely difficult to identify the people who
> benefit from it and to charge them for the benefits which they
> receive. If there is a park in the middle of the city, the houses on
> all sides get the benefit of the green space and people who walk
> through it or by it also benefit. To maintain toll collectors at the
> gates or to impose annual charges per window overlooking the park
> would be very expensive and difficult. The entrances to a national
> park . . . on the other hand, are few, most of the people who come
> stay for a considerable period of time and it is perfectly feasible
> to set up toll gates and collect admission charges.

He makes a similar distinction between general access roads and
long-distance motorways. It is easier to see the administrative reasons
than the ethical grounds for differentiating between city parks and
national parks or city roads and trunk roads.

The third reason for government intervention acceptable to the
anti-collectivists is paternalism for those whom society designates as
not responsible. The severely mentally ill and the severely mentally
handicapped are clear examples — they can neither look after
themselves nor can voluntary agencies manage to care for them. The
State has no option, therefore, but to look after them. The only other
option is to kill them, for to allow them to roam freely would
disturb the normal members of the community. Other examples
meriting paternalistic protection by the State are less clear-cut. What
is the position, for example, with regard to children? Friedman
feels on less safe ground in the case of children, for he is reluctant to
consider them as not responsible. Moreover, the criterion of
responsibility is not the only one to justify State paternalism.
Friedman feels that minimum financial aid to the destitute is justified
on paternalistic grounds, though it is difficult to see how they can all
be designated as not responsible.

Friedman acknowledges the difficult dilemma of accepting
government action on paternalistic grounds. It is difficult to draw the
line between responsible and irresponsible people and the wider the
definition of the term, the more difficult it becomes for
anti-collectivists to criticise the 'paternalistic welfare state' which
they see as undermining individual responsibility and other related
virtues. As a result, the anti-collectivists accept the very same
principle as their opponents, i.e. 'that some shall decide for others'.
Friedman tries to escape his dilemma by putting his faith 'in a
consensus reached by imperfect and biased men through free

discussion and trial and error'.[51]

The welfare state

The welfare state, the anti-collectivists argue, has been fraudulently created by well-meaning, but misguided, reformers capitalising on the rising aspirations of an unthinking general public. The welfare state is, in embryo, a socialist state – it has all the characteristics of a centrally planned and authoritarian socialist society. The historical paradox is that though the general public in the Western world has rejected socialism as a system because of the realisation that, compared with modern capitalism, it is less efficient, it intensifies social stratification and it leads to a new type of despotism, argues Hayek, this same public has accepted the welfare state. Why? Primarily because 'though the characteristic methods of collective socialism have few defenders left in the West, its ultimate aims have lost little of their attraction'.[52] The political means have been rejected but the political ends have been retained.

The public is more prepared to accept piecemeal welfare reforms than political changes on a grand scale because they are presented by reformers as necessary to alleviate particular social ills rather than to change the entire social and economic system. In this way the public can have its cake and eat it – it feels that its cherished traditional way of life is largely preserved and that anomalies in the working of the system are at the same time rectified. Neither the reformers nor the general public look at social problems dispassionately with the result that short-term solutions have been applied without much thought to possible long-term undesirable consequences. It has been a policy of the short-sighted leading the blind. The zealous social reformer demanding immediate State action is short-sighted because by doing so, he may probably prevent the gradual growth of better alternative solutions through the operation of the private market. In fact, the welfare state is economically less efficient than capitalism or socialism where central planning is openly used with all the backing of the government for quick results. As a half-way house, the welfare state combines elements of capitalism and socialism and it is consequently less efficient than either of them.

Powell's explanation of the rise of the welfare state has much in common with Hayek's. It is less subtle but it has the same individualistic ring about it. Looking for an answer to the question why the welfare state has taken such a dangerously strong hold in this country, he postulates thus: 'One danger is that people may simply not know, or not believe, what Socialism is. The other danger is deeper, more insidious, more difficult to combat. It is that only through loss of confidence in themselves could the British people be tempted to go bankrupt and pass over the management of their affairs to an official receiver in the shape of State Socialism.'[53] The promises of Socialism have 'a superficial simplicity and attractiveness',[54] that the general public may find difficult to resist. Every step taken in the direction of Socialism makes it that much more difficult to reverse that trend. What also appears to grieve the anti-collectivists is that all this trouble is heaped on to society not by evil men but by 'men of good intentions and goodwill who wish to reform us'.[55] This process of gradual social reform has gone so far that a general consensus on the welfare state has come to prevail among the public as well as the major political parties in this country, writes Powell. The public has been 'brain-washed' for years into believing that the continual rise in public expenditure cannot be reversed. This frame of mind, he warns, 'is the perfect breeding ground for Socialism'.[56] Even the Conservative Party has come to accept that when in power it cannot dismantle the welfare state in spite of its ideological commitment to free enterprise and vigorous capitalism. The result is that 'every Conservative feels a gnawing sense of contradiction: he proclaims capitalism but acquiesces in Socialism'.[57] The general fear is that 'though Socialism has been generally abandoned as a goal to be deliberately striven for, it is by no means certain that we shall not establish it, albeit unintentionally'.[58]

Though none of our three writers would like to feel that this process is either inevitable or unstoppable, they all agree that it is so entrenched that it needs a major effort to halt it, let alone to reverse it. The trend of increased government intervention has not only been taking place for a long time but it has been accelerating for the last ten years or so, with the result that 'it begins to look as if it were irresistible, as though the wheel could turn only this one way. Unlike a pendulum, which exhausts its force the further it goes in one direction, the effect is cumulative.'[59] Alarmed at this process, which they consider to be 'The Road to Serfdom', they can see no changes in the economic or social system that will change its direction. In a sense, they see themselves as the protagonists, as the clarion-callers of a movement to do just this. It follows naturally from their individualistic interpretation of historical development. As a politician, Powell does this better than the others. Castigating those who passively submit to increased public expenditure and who are trapped into believing in its inevitability, he proclaims: 'All I say is: there is a choice, the choice is open, and it is yours. Let no one cheat you out of your right to take part in that choice, to make your voice heard on one side or the other by telling you that there is no choice at all and the thing is impossible.'[60]

None of our three writers considers the welfare state as a necessary phase to be passed through at a particular stage of industrialisation. They all acknowledge that all industrially developed societies in the West are saddled with welfare states but they do not argue that this was either necessary or inevitable. In fact, the contrary is the case. The creation of the welfare state was both unnecessary and detrimental. In this they part company with many other anti-collectivists. All anti-collectivists are agreed, however, that whatever the origins and whatever the functional necessity of the welfare state may have been in the past, it is now an anachronism, it is perilously close to Socialism and the sooner the trend is reversed to a private market-dominated society, the better for all of us.

We can now look in more detail at the anti-collectivists' criticisms of individual social services. As was discussed earlier in this chapter, the anti-collectivists' notion of the welfare state stems from their acceptance of paternalism and neighbourhood effects as good reasons for government intervention in societal affairs. Though these two principles of government intervention are elastic, they are interpreted by anti-collectivists in a narrow and restricted way. It is, therefore, true to say that anti-collectivists want a reduction of the activities of the welfare state in three main directions. First, they want a reduction as regards the scope of the social services, i.e. the number of people they attempt to help and the areas of people's lives they minister to. This would, in practice, mean that either all social services or large sections of some or all services should be passed over to private provision. Second, they want a reduction in the level of financial benefits the services provide. The State should provide benefits at the minimum level only and leave it to individuals to make better provision for themselves if they so wish. Third, they want a change in the method of administration, i.e. a movement from government to privately administered services or from central government to local government services. Such diffusion and decentralisation of central government powers is desirable because they provide more foci of power and thus greater guarantee of individualism and freedom. In this, anti-collectivists adopt the logic of Ortega's phrase that 'Liberty and Plurality are Reciprocal'.[61]

It is a residual, means-tested or income-tested, locally administered conception of the welfare state. Reviewing the Hobart papers of the Institute of Economic Affairs, Hutchinson writes that the main thrust of their attack 'consists in advocating and advancing the use of pricing and market mechanisms or competitive forces, based on an underlying philosphy which starts from a strong preference for the decentralisation of initiative or for the revival or extension of freedom of choice, for individuals as buyers, sellers or consumers and producers'.[62]

There is general agreement that government intervention in housing has worsened rather than improved the situation. Powell refers to the two Giant Evils of rent control and subsidy that are responsible for the shortage and the other social ills in housing. Hayek is in agreement and they both give the same explanation of why rent control and housing subsidy are to blame for the housing problems. Powell puts it like this: 'You have only to reduce the price of anything below the point at which current supply and demand balance to create shortage in the present and repress production in the future.'[63] In addition, subsidised housing reduces geographical mobility with the result that housing provision no longer corresponds to the needs and the desires of the people. To Hayek, the psychological damage caused by subsidised housing is more serious than the material damage: 'Because of rent restriction, large sections of the population in Western countries have become subject to arbitrary decisions of authority in their daily affairs and accustomed to looking for permission and direction in the main decisions of their lives.'[64] This frame of mind is unhealthy for democracy.

What then is the answer to the housing problem? We must go back to basic economics: 'The same mechanism which provides food, clothing, furniture, carpets, cars, etc. and has done so on an ever-rising standard for everybody, could provide houses too.'[65] All controls and subsidies on housing must, therefore, be abolished as quickly as possible and all council houses must be sold to private companies and to owner-occupiers. This will reduce rates and taxes and will also channel more resources into housing. For the minority of people who may find commercial rents too high, there should be means-tested social security benefits to help them. In brief, 'there ought not to be "a housing policy" any more than there is a food policy, a clothing policy, a furniture and carpets policy, a passenger cars policy and so on.'[66]

Education presents more complicated issues to the anti-collectivists than housing. They start with the basic assumption that compulsory education up to a certain standard is justified on the grounds of 'neighbourhood effects' to use Friedman's phrase or for two reasons, to use Hayek's arguments. These two reasons are 'the general argument that all of us will be exposed to less risks and will receive more benefits from our fellows if they share with us certain basic knowledge and beliefs. And in a country with democratic institutions, there is the further important consideration that democracy is unlikely to work, except on the smallest scale, with a partly illiterate people.'[67] Beyond this minimum standard, which is generally felt to cover primary and secondary education, the responsibility of the State varies depending on whether one is considering vocational or non-vocational education. The arguments cited above do not justify State subsidies to vocational education which increases the earning power of the student. Vocational education must be financed privately and the most the State should do is to provide loans to the most promising students though even this limited scheme is fraught with practical difficulties. As for non-vocational education, the State is justified in providing subsidies because such education benefits the community at large as much, if not more, than the recipients. The important point, however, is that would-be students of higher education have no claim to State subsidies as of right — it is a charitable act on behalf of the State to confer subsidies on the few who show promise. The selection of these few, argues Hayek, must be done in such a way as to represent the various religious, occupational, ethnic and local groups. These students may eventually become leaders of the general community, spokesmen of their particular group, or both.

If the State is justified in making primary and secondary education compulsory for all, it is not justified in being responsible for the actual provision and administration of educational institutions. True, it must provide minimum standards that all educational institutions must observe but their actual provision and administration must be left to private enterprise, except in remote areas of the country, where, because of the small number of children, it would be uneconomic for private enterprise to operate. Parents can choose which schools to send their children to, thus maximising consumer demand to the benefit of all concened — the institutions, the parents and the children. This is based on the basic economic premise of the anti-collectivists that the price and profit mechanisms achieve better results than freely provided social services because of their effects on incentives, competition and choice. Since, however, the State deemed it necessary to make primary and secondary education compulsory, it must also provide financial aid to parents. Friedman and Hayek suggest the provision of vouchers which can be cashed at government approved schools of their choice. These vouchers will be of a specified annual amount that would be sufficient for the fees of some schools but not for others. Parents wishing to send their children to more expensive schools will need to 'top-up' the vouchers. Powell refrains from associating himself with the voucher system though he is in agreement with the other proposals. Friedman is, perhaps, the most enthusiastic exponent of these educational proposals. He feels that the implementation of these proposals far from increasing inequality would, in fact, reduce it. Such a policy[68]

> would make capital more widely available and would thereby do much to make equality of opportunity a reality, to diminish inequalities of income and wealth and to promote the full use of our human resources. And it would do so not by impeding competition, destroying incentive and dealing with symptoms, as would result from the outright redistribution of income, but by strengthening competition, making incentives effective and eliminating the causes of inequality.

Anti-collectivists are agreed that the State has a duty to relieve poverty on grounds of charity and neighbourhood effects. They see this form of government activity as a necessary evil rather than as a positive step to reduce inequalities. In pre-industrial societies voluntary, charitable effort dealt with the problem of poverty but in complex industrial societies this is no longer possible and it becomes the responsibility of the State. The amount of relief must be the lowest acceptable in a particular society and judging from the general tone of the discussion, below the level of flat rate social security benefits. No indication is given, as to what precise considerations are to be taken into account to arrive at the socially acceptable level of poverty. Beyond this level, the State should have no part to play. It is the responsibility of the individual to make his own private provisions for a standard of living that is beyond the minimum. Payment of minimum benefits must be based on a system of means tests. The payment of a benefit to all, irrespective of need, is considered totally unjustifiable, while the application of a means test is considered natural and just. The application of the means test can be made in a purely administrative way in Friedman's scheme of negative income tax. Yet the payment of benefits to all in need through a non-stigmatising process has implications for people's willingness to work hard and to make provision for themselves. To reduce these disincentive effects, Friedman suggests only a 50 per cent rate of subsidy. Even then, it will reduce incentives but not as much as a 100 per cent subsidy. 'Like any other measures to alleviate poverty, it reduces the incentives of those helped to help themselves but it does not eliminate that incentive entirely, as a system of supplementing incomes up to some fixed minimum would. An extra dollar earned always means more money available for expenditure.'[69]

The insurance principle is roundly rejected. It has been used by reformers, argue the anti-collectivists, as a Trojan horse to introduce Socialist legislation. It has led to vertical redistribution of income and by its complexity, it has confused public discussion on the relevant issues. As Powell put it, the camouflaging of taxation as insurance 'has tended to prevent, and still prevents, the main issues from being grasped and properly debated'.[70] Moreover, 'there never was and never could be any link between the pension received and the contribution paid: the whole thing was spoof.'[71] Friedman, too, feels that compulsory State insurance schemes are undesirable. Insurance for retirement pensions[72]

> has deprived all of us of control over a sizable fraction of our income requiring us to devote it to a particular purpose, purchase of a retirement annuity, in a particular way, by buying it from a government concern. It has inhibited competition in the sale of annuities and the development of retirement arrangements. It has given birth to a large bureaucracy that shows tendencies of growing by what it feeds on, of extending its scope from one area of our life to another. And all this, to avoid the danger that a few people might become charges on the public.

Earnings related benefits are equally strongly rejected. In the first place 'the State reduced the individual's power and responsibility for laying out his income',[73] by taking up a large portion of his income to finance such benefits. It also means that the State not only provides benefits to all irrespective of need – a policy which the anti-collectivists condemn – but it also pays more to those least in need. Finally, it is part of the slippery road towards Socialism because it makes everyone dependent on the State and hence increasingly prone to demand more and more State protection. Hayek feels so strongly about present-day schemes of retirement pensions that he fears that unless the trend for increasingly higher pensions at lower retirement ages is halted, the young, who supply the police and the army, will decide the issue: 'concentration camps for the aged unable to maintain themselves are likely to be the fate of an old generation whose income is entirely dependent on coercing the young.'[74]

Anti-collectivists are clearly against a national health service which is free of charge at the point of use. The most government intervention they will accept in this field is for State compulsion on all individuals to insure themselves against sickness with private insurance societies. This is a necessary evil because 'many who could thus provide for themselves might otherwise become a public charge'.[75] Ideally they imply that they would prefer, however, the provision as well as the use of the health service to be left to the decision of individuals. Friedman makes no reference to the health service, though if one can judge from his comments on State insurance schemes for retirement pensions, he would be against a State national health service. Hayek is not explicit about the kind of arrangements he would prefer with regard to health though he is very explicit about what he does not approve. Powell, though against the national health service in principle, is prepared to tolerate it in practice, because of the wide public support it commands and the absence, at present, of strong competition from the private sector.

What are the particular reasons, apart from the general arguments, against the welfare state, for which anti-collectivists are against a national health service? 'One of the strongest arguments against them (free health service schemes)', writes Hayek, 'is, indeed, that their introduction is the kind of politically irrevocable measure that will have to be continued, whether it proves a mistake or not.'[76] He is himself convinced that a national health service is a fundamental mistake for three reasons: First, the extent of medical treatment needed by an individual is unpredictable and can be unlimited as medical science progresses. This must lead to rising costs and hence to rising taxes on all individuals if the health service is to cope with the demand. The result of this must be that the average standard of service that can be provided for all must be low since there is a limit to how much can be raised by government taxation. Second, a national health service does not so much lead to restoring people to working capacity as to prolonging life and alleviating suffering, particularly among the elderly. From the economic point of view this is obviously undesirable, even if from the humanitarian point of view it may be desirable.[77]

> It may seem harsh, but it is probably in the interest of all that under a free system, those with full earning capacity should often be rapidly cured of a temporary and not dangerous disablement at the expense of some neglect of the aged and mortally ill. Where systems of State medicine operate, we generally find that those who could be promptly restored to full activity have to wait for long periods because all the hospital facilities are taken up by people who will never again contribute to the needs of the rest.

Third, at a time when medical knowledge is increasing rapidly, doctors will, under a national health scheme, become State employees obliged to divulge information to the State about their patients, that can be used by the State as it wishes. Such a trend, fears Hayek, 'opens frightening prospects'.[78]

Lees, in one of the Institute of Economic Affairs papers, is in agreement with Hayek. He makes it clear that the fundamental issue of whether medical care should be based on market principles or be made the subject of collective bargaining 'is not something that can be decided on technical grounds; the issue lies beyond economics and derives ultimately from one's beliefs of what constitutes the good society'.[79] The basic value judgment he refers to 'is that the supply of goods and services, including medical care, should as nearly as possible be based upon individual preferences'.[80] It is one of the fundamental canons of anti-collectivists that, to quote Lees again, the market is 'the superior means of registering preferences'.[81]

In general, then, the anti-collectivists are convinced that free and universal social services are ill-conceived and that they cannot possibly achieve their good intentions because of 'the accompanying ill-effects on quality of service caused by public monopoly in supply, on chronic shortage caused by removal of price, on incentives to work caused by the consequent burden of taxation and on consumer freedom caused by the suppression of choice'.[82]

Anti-collectivists hope that their fellow citizens will acknowledge the economic and political risks involved in the mixed economy of the welfare state and will reverse the trend to competitive capitalism before the welfare state imperceptibly leads us down the road to serfdom and into the Socialist State.

3

THE RELUCTANT COLLECTIVISTS

Social values

In many respects the values of the reluctant collectivists are similar
to those of the anti-collectivists. Both groups emphasise their
belief in liberty, in individualism and in competitive private enterprise.
The reluctants, however, hold fewer absolute values. Their values
tend to be conditional and to be qualified by their intellectual
pragmatism.

Their pragmatism is the product of the conviction that capitalism
is not self-regulating. They continue to believe that capitalism is the
best economic system, but they believe that to function efficiently
and fairly it requires judicious regulation and control. Its faults are
serious, but not fundamental; they can be corrected. 'You have made
yourself', Keynes wrote to President Roosevelt in his famous Open
Letter in December 1933, 'the trustee for those in every country who
seek to mend the evils of our condition by reasoned experiment, within
the framework of our existing social system.'[1] This was the aim and
ideal of the reluctant collectivists.

Their pragmatism leads the reluctants to the view that the nature
and limits of state action cannot be settled on abstract grounds of
principle, but must be determined on their merits in specific cases.[2]
There was no single way of achieving full employment, Beveridge
argued. The only answer lay in 'a selective combination of methods; we
need various types of general control . . . we need probably public
monopoly ownership in certain fields, private enterprise subject to
public control in other fields, private enterprise free of any save the

42

general controls in yet other fields.'[3] Galbraith's conclusion was
that 'no natural superiority can be assumed either for the market
or for planning . . . . The error is in basing action on generalisation.'[4]
In the past, the choice between capitalism and socialism was
ideological. Today that is not so. 'The new socialism is not ideological;
it is compelled by circumstance.'[5]

This pragmatism is underpinned by a strong humanism. It was
concern about the human implications of capitalism which led
Keynes, Beveridge and Galbraith in their different periods, and for
very different reasons, to explore the nature of an economic system
which seemed so hurtful to so many.[6] Concern about unemployment
was the inspiration of Keynes's major work. Though he had many
typically Conservative characteristics, his concern about social ills and
his sensitivity to suffering led him to question the conventional
economic orthodoxies.[7] Beveridge's fundamental humanism comes
out most clearly in his definition of full employment. It means, he
said, that there will always be more vacant jobs than there are men
without work, that the labour market should be a seller's rather than
a buyer's market. The buyer who has difficulty in purchasing labour
suffers inconvenience or some reduction in his profits, whereas the
seller who can find no market for his labour is told in effect that
he is of no use. 'The first difficulty causes annoyance or loss. The
other is a personal catastrophe.'[8] In Beveridge's eyes, the greatest
evil of unemployment was not the loss of additional material
wealth involved, but the fact that 'unemployment makes men seem
useless, not wanted, without a country'.[9] Keynes and Beveridge
would both have accepted Galbraith's judgment that society's
highest task is 'to reflect on its pursuit of happiness and harmony
and its success in expelling pain, tension, sorrow, and the ubiquitous
curse of ignorance'.[10]

Freedom and liberty are fundamental values for the reluctants.
After first reading 'The Road to Serfdom', Keynes wrote to Hayek
that 'Morally and philosophically I find myself in agreement with
virtually the whole of it, and not only in agreement with it, but in
a deeply moved agreement.'[11] He went on, however, to disassociate
himself from Hayek's views on planning. Beveridge stressed on many
occasions that his aim was full employment in a free society. He
regarded certain liberties as essential — freedom of worship, speech,
writing, study and teaching, freedom of assembly and association for
political or other purposes, freedom in choice of occupation and
freedom in the management of a personal income.[12] They were 'more
precious than full employment itself'.[13] Beveridge's approach to
questions of freedom was essentially pragmatic. Control of the
location of industry, he argued, is a restriction of freedom but 'It is

better, and less of an interference with individual lives, to control business men in the location of their enterprises than to leave them uncontrolled and require workpeople to move their homes for the sake of employment. Control by the State of location of industry is the alternative both to the compulsory direction of labour and to the making of distressed areas.'[14] Beveridge also saw what the anti-collectivists tend to forget or ignore, that 'Liberty means more than freedom from the arbitrary power of governments. It means freedom from economic servitude to Want and Squalor and other social evils.'[15]

The reluctant collectivists lay great stress on individualism, private enterprise and self-help. These beliefs are what underlie their preference for capitalism over other forms of economic organisation. Keynes speaks of 'the traditional advantages of individualism' and proceeds to describe them.[16]

> They are partly advantages of efficiency — the advantages of decentralisation and of the play of self-interest . . . . But above all, individualism, if it can be purged of its defects and its abuses, is the best safeguard of personal liberty in the sense that, compared with any other system, it greatly widens the field for the exercise of personal choice. It is also the best safeguard of the variety of life, which emerges precisely from this extended field of personal choice, or the loss of which is the greatest of all the losses of the homogeneous or totalitarian state.

Individualism and private enterprise were important to Keynes for two other reasons. Like Dicey and Hayek, he saw them as vital sources of innovation and initiative — 'New forms and modes spring from the fruitful minds of individuals', as he put it. He also believed in 'the deep wisdom in those seventeenth and eighteenth century thinkers who discovered and preached a profound connection between personal and political liberty and the rights of private property and private enterprise'.[17]

Beveridge shared Keynes's views. 'The State', he wrote, 'is or can be master of money, but in a free society it is master of very little else. The making of a good society depends not on the State but on the citizens acting individually or in free association with one another.'[18] Beveridge's proposals to secure and maintain full employment had the aim, as he put it, 'of keeping private enterprise as servant not as master'.[19]

In their attitude to equality and inequality the reluctant collectivists separate themselves very clearly from the Fabian socialists and the Marxists. They are not egalitarians though they do think that inequalities should and could be reduced. Keynes was unashamedly elitist in his thinking. In his view, says Harrod, 'the first claim upon the national dividend was to furnish those few, who were capable of "passionate perception", with the ingredients of what modern civilisation can provide by way of a "good life".'[20]

Keynes's defence of inequality had two central elements — social and psychological. His social argument was that 'there are valuable human activities which require the motive of money making and the environment of private wealth ownership for their full fruition.' His psychological justification was rather more eccentric. 'Dangerous human proclivities', he thought, 'can be canalised into comparatively harmless channels by the existence of opportunities for money making and private wealth, which, if they cannot be satisfied in this way, may find their outlet in cruelty, the reckless pursuit of personal power and authority, and other forms of self-aggrandisement.'[21] It was not necessary, however, in Keynes's view, that 'the game should be played for such high stakes as at present.'[22]

Beveridge also stressed the economic functions of inequality. Without differences of reward to allocate manpower there would have to be direction of labour. 'Economic rewards for effort and economic punishment for failure of effort', he concluded, 'are the alternative to the chain gang.'[23] At the same time, he pressed the moral and economic case for greater equality. The moral argument is that the same amount of wealth will yield more happiness if it is distributed widely rather than if it is concentrated. The economic case is that more equal distribution of wealth and income will increase aggregate demand and so contribute towards the goal of full employment. Galbraith shares the view that inequalities of income should be reduced. But he does not wish to see differentials eliminated. The elimination of poverty is, in his view, a far more important issue than a search for a chimerical equality.[24]

Society and the State

The reluctant collectivists' analysis of society concentrates almost entirely on the economic system. Being basically conservative, they accept the social and political order as given. They have little to say about class and only Galbraith includes any real discussion of power. Their criticisms of capitalism can be grouped under four main headings: capitalism is not self-regulating; it is wasteful and inefficient and misallocates resources; it will not of itself abolish injustice and poverty; it leads to dominant economic interests being identified as the national interest.

The doctrine of a self-regulating economic system was a very comfortable one. It included two essential articles   that regulatory action by the State was necessary neither on economic grounds nor on political grounds. State action on economic grounds was unnecessary because, according to Say's Law of Markets, production automatically created its own sufficient demand. 'Whether or not a person accepted Say's Law', says Galbraith, 'was, until the 1930s, the prime test by which economists were distinguished from crackpots.'[25]

A self-regulating capitalism raised no political problems either. The consumer was sovereign. Competition ensured that he remained the ultimate authority. Neither consumers nor workers could be exploited because they would simply take their custom or their labour elsewhere. As Galbraith puts it, 'if choice by the public is the source of power, the organisations that comprise the economic system cannot have power. They are merely instruments in the ultimate service of that choice.'[26] The economic system is thus democratised. Ultimate power in economic as well as political affairs rests with the individual. 'The public through the consumer being already in charge, the public through the government need not and should not intervene.'[27]

Keynes was a fierce critic of laissez-faire. 'It is not true', he wrote, 'that individuals possess a prescriptive "natural liberty" in their economic activities. There is no "compact" conferring perpetual rights on those who Have or those who Acquire. The world is not so governed from above that private and social interest always coincide.'[28] But Keynes's great achievement was to destroy the notion of a self-regulating economic system and provide the theoretical underpinning for a new economics. He demonstrated that the inter-war depression was in effect a refutation of Say's Law and showed that there was no technical reason why demand and production should be in balance. Such an analysis, says Stewart, was 'dramatic' and 'imperative', 'dramatic because it stood existing economic theory on its head, imperative because it implied the need for government action of a kind, and on a scale, never before contemplated.'[29]

The notion of a non-self-regulating economy was revolutionary. 'By making it impossible to believe any longer in an automatic reconciliation of conflicting interests into a harmonious whole', says Joan Robinson, 'the General Theory brought out into the open the problem of choice and judgment that the neo-classicals had managed to smother. The ideology to end ideologies broke down. Economics once more became Political Economy.'[30]

Keynes saw the key weakness of the market economy as deficiency of demand. Beveridge's view was that the demand for labour was not merely inadequate but misdirected. He pointed out that between the wars if the demand had been so much greater quantitatively as to equal the available supply but had been directed locally preserving the same proportions between the different regions of Britain, this demand would have failed to abolish unemployment. Beveridge, therefore, wanted government action on three lines — to maintain total outlay at all times, to control the location of industry, and to secure the organised mobility of labour.[31]

Keynes's thinking was about the failure of the unregulated economy to ensure sufficient demand to avoid depression and unemployment. Beveridge had the same preoccupation. Galbraith takes the discussion of the non-self-regulating economy and applies it to the affluent capitalism which is the essential product and achievement of the Keynesian revolution. Given the application of Keynesian techniques of economic management and the achievement of near full employment, Galbraith sees the resulting system as in desperate need of government control and regulation. Keynes hoped that within a proper framework of government economic policy the economic system could again become self-regulating. Galbraith shows that this dream has not come true.

The main thesis which Galbraith has developed so powerfully is that technological development increases industry's need for State help. Industry needs highly trained manpower and it relies on the State to supply it. It needs investment funds for exciting but uncertain projects. The development of new products requires a heavy advance commitment of money, time and manpower. Industry must be able to be confident that there will, in the end, be a market for the product. In this situation, 'The regulation of aggregate demand . . . is an organic requirement of the industrial system.'[32]

In an affluent society State regulation of demand is more necessary than in a poorer society because, with affluence, saving and spending become much more matters for individual and corporate choice and decision. 'In consequence', Galbraith argues, 'in a community of high well-being, spending and hence demand are less reliable than in a poor one. They lose their reliability precisely when high costs and the long period of gestation imposed by modern technology require greater certainty of markets.'[33] The real enemy of the market, therefore, is not socialism but advanced technology.[34]

Galbraith further develops this thesis arguing that in the absence of State intervention the planning system (i.e. the giant corporations) is inherently unstable, subject to recession and depression which are not self-limiting as in simpler economies, but which can become cumulative.[35] In simpler economies there are natural mechanisms which operate to stop the downward movement of economic activity from becoming cumulative. In the planning system these do not operate. Prices do not fall because they are controlled by the firm; wages cannot be reduced because of the strength of the trade unions.

Galbraith has emphasised one further way in which advanced capitalism is not self-regulating – its inability to control inflation. Beveridge anticipated the problem but with the advantage of thirty years' experience of inflation Galbraith has sharpened the analysis. The key factor which makes inflation 'an organic feature of the industrial system',[36] is that prices are now determined not by the market but by the firm. This means that the individual firm will not put up more than a token resistance to wage demands because it can finance them by raising prices. There is no body which can supply general restraint except the State. So there is no alternative to State action.[37]

In Galbraith's view, the recognition that the capitalist system suffered from downward instability was not fatal. The State simply propped up the existing system. A recognition of upward instability implies more fundamental problems because if firms can simply raise prices to meet wage claims, then prices are not subordinate to the market. 'One cannot have a market system in which there is massive wage and price fixing.'[38] The only solution for reasonable men is a system of wage and price control.

Keynes and Beveridge seem to be making very different criticisms of capitalism from Galbraith. In fact, all are concerned to stress capitalism's inability to achieve self-regulation and to suggest how public action can make good this failing without destroying the system. What Harrod said of Keynes could be applied to Beveridge and Galbraith as well. 'His lifelong effort to understand what is wrong with the machine', he wrote, 'implies that he wanted us to continue to use the machine, implies, in fact, that he was at bottom an individualist.'[39]

The second major charge which the reluctant collectivists bring against unregulated capitalism is that it is wasteful and inefficient and leads to an unsatisfactory allocation of resources. Keynes and Beveridge were both appalled by the waste involved in the inter-war depression. 'Failure to use our productive powers', Beveridge stressed, 'is the source of an interminable succession of evils.'[40] As he argued in his social insurance plan, want could have been abolished in the inter-war years had government so willed.[41] Keynes expressed his similar 'profound conviction that the Economic Problem, as one may call it for short, the problem of want and poverty and the economic struggle between classes and nations, is nothing but a frightful muddle, a transitory and an unnecessary muddle.'[42]

For Keynes and Beveridge the problem was an economy which was failing to use its productive capacity to the full. For Galbraith the problem was the use to which a successful economic system was putting its productive capacities. He criticised the 'ubiquitous' and 'obtrusive' contrast between private affluence and public squalor which he saw as inherent in the advanced capitalist economy. Such a contrast, he argued, was not only offensive. It was also dangerous. 'An austere community is free from temptation. It can be austere in its public services. Not so a rich one.'[43] If it is austere, problems of crime, vandalism, violence and drug abuse are more likely to proliferate.

In his more recent writings, Galbraith locates the reasons for this social imbalance firmly in the nature of capitalism. Not all public services, he realised, were deprived of resources. 'This deprivation was great where public needs were involved, non-existent where powerful industry pressed its requirements on the State.'[44] Defence, research and technological development, highways and air traffic management were not neglected because they were demanded by powerful voices. But the care of the ill, the old, the physically and mentally handicapped, the provision of recreational facilities, the problem of poverty were urged by no powerful voices. They were thus neglected.[45]

Another aspect of this imbalance is the contrast between the planning system, the world of the great corporations, and the market system, the world of small, traditional undeveloped industries. The former has embraced and dominates the State. It has succeeded in identifying its interests as the national interest. The latter, which among other things supplies housing, health and urban transport, is weak and ineffective. It lacks the ear of government and is, therefore, without open or hidden public subsidies. Basic human needs are, therefore, met inadequately or inefficiently.

Because of their values, the waste and patterns of allocation of an unregulated capitalism are intolerable to the reluctant collectivists. They do not regard these ills as inevitable but as susceptible to control and elimination by due regulation.

Another concern shared by the reluctant collectivists is their conviction that without government action, economic development will not as a natural outcome of rising general prosperity abolish poverty. Beveridge saw this and emphasised its importance, pointing out that the growing general prosperity and rising real wage levels between 1900 and 1939 had diminished want, but still left a sizeable problem. 'The moral', he concluded, 'is that new measures to spread prosperity are needed.'[46]

Galbraith pointed out the same truth, the argument strengthened by the passing of time and faster growth. Increasing aggregate output, he emphasised 'leaves a self-perpetuating margin of poverty at the very base of the income pyramid'.[47] He urged that an income necessary for decency and comfort should be secured to all 'as a normal function of the society'.[48] He sees the failure of economic growth to abolish poverty as one aspect of the many sided social imbalance inherent in the advanced capitalist economy. By its very nature it generates and perpetuates inequality and poverty.

Galbraith sees as one of the important underlying problems of capitalism the way in which sectional interests come to be equated with the public interest. The sectional interests which dominate in America are those of the planning system. To survive and flourish, advanced capitalism must cultivate an ethos which encourages people to acquire and consume its products. Production, therefore, becomes a god. Industry has the key to the good life if not to the gates of heaven. When industry needs government help, it gets it, because what serves industry and production serves the national interest. The locus of power in the planning system is the technostructure. It is made up of the most prestigious, affluent and articulate members of the community. Their views on public policy, therefore, command immense and solemn respect. 'What serves the technostructure — the protection of its autonomy of decision, the promotion of economic growth, the stabilization of aggregate demand, the acceptance of its claim to superior income, the provision of qualified manpower, the government services and investment that it requires, the other requisites of success — IS the public interest.'[49]

As an example of the power of the planning system, Galbraith instances its success in controlling the nature and direction of Keynesian type economic policies. 'As originally envisaged', he writes, 'the government would intervene with increased civilian expenditure of general public benefit, not covered by taxes, to offset the deficiency of aggregate demand. But following World War II, the Keynesian Resolution was, in effect, absorbed by the planning system. Thereafter, government policy reflected closely the planning system's needs. Public expenditures were set at a permanently high level and extensively concentrated on military and other technical artifacts or on military or industrial development.'[50] Galbraith sees the support given by the State to aggregate demand as simply 'an extension of the power of the planning system'.[51]

The dominance of the planning system and the establishment of its interests as the public interest helps to explain many of the inefficiencies, injustices and other blots on the capitalist copybook. Galbraith sees this colonisation of the State as a major flaw in advanced capitalism and as a major obstacle to be overcome if capitalism is to be reformed.

In spite of these various criticisms, what is required, in the view of the reluctant collectivists, is not that capitalism be superseded, but that it be regulated. 'The necessity of socialism, in the sense of nationalisation of the means of production, distribution and exchange, in order to secure full employment', Beveridge wrote, 'has not yet been demonstrated.'[52] If, however, it was shown that the abolition of private enterprise was necessary to achieve full employment 'this abolition would have to be undertaken.'[53]

Keynes devoted most of his life to criticising the workings of the capitalist system and yet he remained a firm supporter of its fundamental principles. He concluded his fierce attack 'The End of Laissez-Faire' with the reflection that 'capitalism, wisely managed, can probably be made more efficient for attaining economic ends than any alternative system yet in sight' although 'it is in many ways extremely objectionable.'[54] Seymour Harris concluded that 'Keynes's mission in life was to save capitalism, not destroy it.'[55] Galbraith says that Keynes 'sought for nothing so earnestly as to save liberal capitalism'.[56] Keynes saw its faults as technical rather than fundamental. Through appropriate government action he believed that a middle way could be found 'between the anarchy of laissez-faire and the tyranny of totalitarianism'.[57]

Beveridge similarly stressed the non-political nature of his proposals both for social insurance and for securing full employment. They were, he insisted, neither socialism nor capitalism. 'A conscious control of the economic system at the highest level', he insisted, is '. . . required in any modern society.'[58]

Keynes and Beveridge were concerned with the capitalism of the Depression, Galbraith with the capitalism of the affluent society. Their attitudes, however, are remarkably similar. In his early writings, Galbraith could see 'no administratively acceptable alternative to the decision making mechanism of capitalism'.[59] Public ownership would, in comparison, be clumsy and unresponsive, impracticable in the complex economic system of advanced industrial society.

In Galbraith's view, of course, contemporary capitalism is very different from the classical model. Power has passed from owners to managers. 'The decisive power in modern industrial society is exercised not by capital but by organisation, not by the capitalist but by the industrial bureaucrat.'[60] The technostructure — Galbraith's collective term for the industrial-technical bureaucracy — is not, in his view, concerned with the maximisation of profits but rather with maintaining its independence of owners and government, with the safety and survival of the enterprise and with growth.[61]

In his later writings, Galbraith is increasingly critical of many features of capitalism and he has come to believe that for some tasks capitalism is unsatisfactory. It is, for example, 'seriously incompetent in providing the things and services that cities most require . . . the modern city is, by its nature, a socialist enterprise.'[62] Such areas and services must be removed from the capitalist system and governed collectively.

But apart from the pragmatic, un-ideological New Socialism of necessity, Galbraith seems to continue to see capitalism as the main system of distribution. It is to be regarded as normal except when it fails, and then we should be brisk and businesslike, though a shade regretful, and accept socialism as a necessary and wholly normal feature of the system.

The way in which the faults, weaknesses and ills of capitalism are analysed is an important factor in the subsequent proposals. The reluctant collectivists are led by their analysis to the view that all can be made good through government action. Galbraith produces the most up to date and relevant analysis of what is wrong and he is led by it to the most radical proposals but, although again and again he describes the ills of capitalism as 'systemic' (one of his favourite words), he nevertheless clings to the belief that 'systemic', 'inherent', 'organic' ills can be relieved without changes which would destroy or supersede capitalism.

The role of government

Although the anti-collectivists disapprove of some government action of which the Marxists approve, the two groups are united in their doubts about State action; the former because they believe in the inherent superiority of natural forces, the latter because they see the State, not as an independent body concerned for and equipped to further the interests of all, but rather as one of the many forces by which dominant social groups further their interests. The reluctant collectivists and the Fabian socialists are united in their belief in the benevolent potentialities of government action.

A key element in the thinking of the reluctant collectivists is their belief in rational action. They reject the view that the economic and social system is governed by mysterious, self-regulating principles which are best left severely alone. They believe that, by rational thought and planning, problems can be solved. 'He believed', says Harrod of Keynes, 'that, by care and pains, all our social evils, distressed areas, unemployment and the rest, could be abolished. He believed in planning and contriving. A way could be found.'[63] 'Nothing is required', Keynes wrote of the economic situation in 1933, 'and nothing will avail, except a little, a very little, clear thinking.'[64] This belief underlies the analysis and prescriptions of the reluctants. They believe that men can control their economic and social destiny. This gives them the impetus to seek to create a world more in keeping with their values.

Keynes and Beveridge share this view of the State as a body able to take an independent view of the problems presented to it, having regard only to the public interest. Sweezy talks of 'Keynes's habit of treating the State as a deus ex machina to be invoked whenever his human actors, behaving according to the rules of the capitalist game, get themselves into a dilemma from which there is apparently no escape.'[65] There is no sense in which either Keynes or Beveridge see the State as the focus of a range of conflicting interests. They see it as able to stand in an independent role of judgment on the functioning of the economic system, the performance of private enterprise, and the distribution of the national income.

Galbraith does not share their optimism. He is quite clear in 'Economics and the Public Purpose' that the State is in fact the creature of the dominant economic interest, what he styles the planning system. It has been successful in identifying its interests as the public interest. State action, therefore, is in fact geared to the very particular interests of the planning system rather than the general interest. Nevertheless, Galbraith believes that the State can be emancipated from this sectional embrace and be recaptured 'for the public purpose'[66] by a demonstration of the divergence between the planning interest and the public interest and by the inculcation of a new, critical, public awareness.

Although they believe that government has a positive part to play in economic and social life, the reluctant collectivists are keen to emphasise the limitations which they place on government activity. 'As a Radical', Beveridge said in 1945, 'I am not afraid of State control or public ownership where either of these is necessary to cure evils which cannot be cured without them, but my bias is against them not for them.'[67] 'The underlying principle of the Report', he wrote of 'Full Employment', 'is to propose for the State only those things which the State alone can do or which it can do better than any local authority or than private citizens either singly or in association, and to leave to these other agencies that which if they will they can do as well or better than the State.'[68]

Despite Beveridge's stress on the limitations of government, his ideas, as did those of Keynes, implied a major expansion of government activity in a way which was qualitatively new. 'Too much of our economic thinking in the thirties', wrote one reviewer of 'Full Employment', 'awarded to the central government the dual function of running its own affairs and tinkering with the capitalistic system in its spare time. Beveridge's thesis, on the other hand, is that the government, in running its own affairs, cannot ignore the effects of its actions on the capitalistic system, and must adjust its programs so that government and business jointly achieve full employment. The notion of the doctor prescribing for a sick patient is discarded in favour of the principle of partnership, with the qualification that the government is responsible if things go wrong.'[69] Beveridge was torn between his suspicion and dislike of government and his passionate determination to destroy the five Giants. His liberal principles led him to seek to stress the limitations which he believed should be applied to government action, while on the other hand, his passionate concern about social ills led him at times to the view that many less essential liberties could rightly and reasonably be sacrificed to their abolition.

Like Beveridge, Keynes believed that government activity should be confined to achieving these results which could not be secured by unco-ordinated individual effort. 'The most important Agenda of the State', he wrote, 'relate not to those activities which private individuals are already fulfilling but to the functions which fall outside the sphere of the individual, to those decisions which are made by no one if the State does not make them. The important thing for government is not to do things which individuals are doing already, and to do them a little better or a little worse; but to do those things which at present are not done at all.'[70] Over the years, Keynes became more accepting of government intervention in social and economic life but this remained his basic position. To combine stress on the necessity and inevitability of government intervention and activity with stress on its limitation is, however, difficult. As Galbraith pointed out, Keynes 'though unobtrusively, opened the way for a large expansion of government services and activities.'[71]

Galbraith has a much wider view of the necessary sphere of State action than Keynes or Beveridge. In his view, the lines of economic and social development have greatly widened the area in which collectivist solutions must be applied. But it is still a reluctant and limited collectivism confined to issues where the normal solutions of private enterprise and the free market have been unsuccessful. It is a collectivism not of principle, but of necessity.

The reluctant collectivists, therefore, believe in limiting the role of government because of their belief in the ability of a free market system to regulate itself once a framework has been established, because of their belief in the natural superiority of private enterprise as a source of initiative and a bastion of liberty, and because of their suspicion that government action is a potential threat to freedom at the same time as they see it as necessary to freedom. The views of the reluctant collectivists on the role of government can usefully be examined in more detail in relation to economic, social and physical planning.

They are agreed on the duty and responsibility of government to manage the economy so as to secure a level of aggregate demand which will ensure full employment. Keynes defended such action 'both as the only practicable means of avoiding the destruction of existing economic forms in their entirety and as the condition of the successful functioning of individual initiative.'[72] Beveridge similarly urged the responsibility of the State to maintain adequate total outlay and emphasised that this must be seen as a function of the State 'as definitely as it is now the function of the State to defend its citizens against attack from abroad or against robbery and violence at home.'[73] The State must assume this responsibility because 'no other authority or person has the requisite powers.'[74]

Keynes's basic concern was with economic management to provide a framework in which natural forces could operate. Beveridge is much more concerned with economic planning for social goals. He rejects certain approaches because they are socially unacceptable. The use of public investment to compensate for fluctuations in private investment is unacceptable because communal investment is too important to be kept on tap to fill gaps in private spending.[75] On similar grounds, Beveridge rejects a simple expansion of private outlay approach as the whole answer. Such a policy is unlikely to be effective, he thinks, and it does nothing about the problem that there are many essential services which individuals either cannot get for themselves or can only get at excessive cost compared with the cost of collective provision.[76]

Keynes's work gave a new legitimacy to public expenditure. The traditional neo-classical view was that any expansion of public expenditure above what was directly necessary to the functioning of private enterprise, was dangerous. This was because such investment absorbed funds which would otherwise have been profitably invested in industry. If, as Keynes argued, desired savings could exceed desired investment, then public expenditure was no longer at the expense of private investment, and was not by definition bad and wasteful.[77]

The question of the maintenance of aggregate demand could not in practice be separated from questions of distribution. Keynes pointed out in 'The General Theory' that savings by institutions and sinking funds were more than adequate as a source of capital and, therefore, 'measures for the redistribution of incomes, in a way likely to raise the propensity to consume, may prove positively favourable to the growth of capital.' Such distribution, of course, would be more equal. If the depression of the economy arises from an excess of saving 'One of the chief social justifications of greater inequality of wealth is, therefore, removed.'[78]

Management of the economy to secure full employment has other implications for the wider role of State action. 'Adoption by the State of a price policy', Beveridge reckoned, 'is a natural and probably an inevitable consequence of a full employment policy.'[79] Galbraith has developed the argument and sees State regulation of wages and prices as the only way to combat the inflationary tendencies inherent in the fully employed corporate State.[80]

Galbraith also believes that intervention to reduce inequality of development between the planning and the market system is a responsibility of the State. For some industries and services, the solution is the New Socialism, for others the setting of minimum wages and guaranteed incomes will be sufficient. Alongside this compensatory role, Galbraith sets the controlling role of curbing the planning system so that it serves rather than defines the public interest. 'Rules of the road' and the stabilisation or socialisation of demand are not adequate solutions to the problems which have followed full employment and technological development. The logic of developments points to a wider economic responsibility for government.

As regards planning for social welfare purposes, it is necessary to make only a few general points here as the attitude of the reluctant collectivists to the welfare responsibilities of government will be discussed in more detail later. The reluctant collectivists see the responsibility of the government as starting from those social tasks considered to be necessary, but only attainable through government action. 'There are vital things needing to be done to raise the standard of health and happiness in Britain', said Beveridge, 'which can only be done by common action.'[81] 'We cannot overcome social evils', he urged elsewhere, 'without an extension of the responsibilities of the State.'[82] The inter-war economy, to which Beveridge looked back with such distaste, was characterised by two major ills — unused productive resources and crying social evils. Economic planning was aimed at the first, social planning at the second. The State must take the lead because it is the only body which can co-ordinate the onslaught on the giants blocking the road to reconstruction. They must be conquered because their domination means tyranny and misery which are bad in themselves and bad too because 'Misery generates hate'.

Only the State can make decisions about social priorities. Beveridge described his plan for social insurance as 'a practical programme for putting first things first. There was to be bread and health for all at all times before cake and circuses for anybody at any time.'[83] Only the State can set such guidelines. Only the State, too, can co-ordinate social and economic policies. If the State assumes the responsibility for maintaining full employment, this does not remove the need for social insurance. Similarly, social insurance on its own 'is so inadequate a provision for human happiness that to put it forward by itself as a sole or principal measure of reconstruction hardly seems worth doing.'[84] It was only when economic policies for full employment were combined with policies to mitigate the suffering resulting from inevitable interruptions of earnings that effective planning could be said to take place.

Galbraith stresses the responsibility of the government to achieve social balance and to ensure that the affluence of the private sector is matched by a public sector of comparable resources. His thesis is that affluence increases rather than reduces the need for public expenditure and provision.

Galbraith also wants to use government action as a lever to raise wage levels. He argues for the fixing of a guaranteed income for those who cannot find employment, at a level 'modestly below what can be earned in the planning system', where, of course, earnings are considerably higher than in the market system. The object of this is to set 'a limit below which wages in the market system cannot be reduced.'[85] It is a key purpose of the scheme 'that an individual not be forced to reduce his income below some minimum in order to get that work.'[86] If, as a result, certain industries and activities go out of business this should be no cause for regret.

The reluctant collectivists, therefore, see government responsibility for social planning as embracing five elements — the attack on manifest social ills, the mitigation of social imbalance, a setting of social priorities, co-ordination with economic planning and as a stimulus to private enterprise.

Beveridge's concern for physical planning was an aspect of his wider concerns. To achieve full employment 'control over the location of industry is indispensable.'[87] Regional and structural unemployment could only be limited by the direction of new industrial development to the distressed areas. He accepted such control as a restriction of liberty but saw it as one of those less essential liberties worth sacrificing for full employment.

Similarly if Giant Squalor was to be vanquished, Beveridge believed the planned use of land was vital. 'We must be in a position to ensure', he wrote, 'that the use of all land in the country is determined according to a national plan, and not just by individual bargaining between two citizens, one owning and one meaning to use a particular piece of land.'[88]

Galbraith is concerned for public physical planning where the market fails. In the urban land market this leads him to advocate public land acquisition.[89] In relation to the environment, he sees it as a responsibility of government to set 'explicit and unyielding legal specifications' to control pollution, with full autonomy for industry within this framework. Galbraith's approach is essentially utilitarian. Products, services and technology 'where the social cost and discomfort are deemed to outweigh the individual advantages' should be banned.[90] State action is required to protect the community from the consequences of innumerable quite legitimate individual decisions which become intolerable when aggregated.

The welfare state

Keynes had little to say directly about what we think of as the welfare state, though he was clearly sympathetic towards an extension of welfare services. In 1930, when discussing methods of improving the conditions of the working class, he spoke for an increase in social service provision rather than a rise in wages as the next step in advance.[91] Harrod says that the general philosophy of the Beveridge Report on Social Insurance accorded with Keynes's views and that he gave 'warm general support to the Beveridge proposals', though he persuaded Beveridge to reduce the commitment of the Exchequer in the early years.[92] It would have pleased Keynes as a humanitarian concerned for the abolition of avoidable social ills and it would have fitted his pleas for a redistribution of purchasing power to those most likely to spend.

For both Beveridge and Galbraith individual welfare was their ultimate concern. Subject to the preservation of essential liberties, Beveridge was prepared 'to use the powers of the State, so far as may be necessary without any limit whatever, in order to abolish the five giant evils'.[93] We must regard the five giants, Want, Disease, Ignorance, Squalor and Idleness, he stressed, as common enemies, not as enemies with which each individual may seek a separate peace. 'That is the meaning of social conscience; that one should refuse to make a separate peace with social evil.'[94] Galbraith's whole critique of American capitalism is rooted and grounded in the belief that it does not serve individual welfare or the public interest. His aim is for a State concerned for welfare, the public interest and the good life — a welfare state.

Beveridge and Galbraith share a pragmatic approach to the role of the State in welfare. It is to abolish avoidable ills; the role is to be reactive rather than promotional; it is problem centred. Their concern is to supply what is not being supplied adequately by private enterprise, to abolish want whether due to low or interrupted incomes, and, in Galbraith's case, to supply the public services for which affluence has created a need.

Beveridge's stress was on the achievement of a national minimum. He would have endorsed the sentiments of his former political master that 'We want to draw a line below which we will not allow persons to live and labour, yet above which they may compete with all the strength of their manhood. We want to have free competition upwards; we decline to allow free competition to run downwards.'[95] The aim of Beveridge's plan for social insurance was quite simply 'to make want under any circumstances unnecessary'.[96] 'In the total outlay directed to maintaining full employment, priority is required for a minimum for all citizens of housing, health, education and nutrition, and a minimum of investment to raise the standard of life of future generations.'[97] It was definitely not, however, the responsibility of government to provide more than a minimum. Compulsory contributions to provide more than a minimum would, in Beveridge's view, be an attack on the individual's freedom to spend his money as he thinks best.[98] A national minimum both abolished want and preserved the individual's liberty to provide, or not to provide, benefits for himself and his family over and above this.

Galbraith was prepared to go farther than Beveridge and establish a guaranteed minimum income for those not at work which would force employers to raise wages to this level.[99] Beveridge was, of course, concerned with a subsistence minimum, Galbraith with relative poverty rather than subsistence, but Galbraith's willingness to use such a powerful weapon to raise low pay is in line with Beveridge's view that the State should use all available powers to abolish want subject only to the preservation of essential liberties.

Beveridge's main weapon in the struggle to secure a national minimum was insurance. Insurance appealed to Beveridge for a variety of reasons. Social insurance raised no party political issues and this gave his plan a strong chance of being implemented. But the key argument in favour of contributory insurance, in Beveridge's view, was that it was the only way to secure benefits as of right without a means test.[100] The avoidance of a means test was very important because such tests discourage voluntary insurance and saving. Thrift is important in itself and it is economically important if a larger proportion of the total savings of the community are going to have to come in the future from the modest savings of many citizens, rather than from the immodest savings of the few. To stimulate thrift basic benefits must be granted without a means test.[101] A contributory scheme is also important to avoid the idea that the State is the dispenser of gifts for which no one needs to pay – a bottomless philanthropic purse. Writing of Family Allowances, Beveridge expressed the view that 'The principle of social policy should not be to remove all responsibilities from parents, but to help them to understand and to meet their responsibilities.'[102] This also aptly expresses his view of the value of social insurance.

What did Beveridge see as the respective roles of social and voluntary insurance? Social insurance 'should not leave either to national assistance or to voluntary insurance any risk so general or so uniform that social insurance can be justified.' The disadvantage of national assistance is that it involves a means test and so discourages voluntary insurance or personal saving. Voluntary insurance on the other hand 'can never be sure of covering the ground' and is also more expensive to administer.[103]

But Beveridge regarded voluntary insurance as a vital element in his plan. It was essential that the State scheme 'should leave room and encouragement for voluntary action by each individual to provide more than that minimum for himself and his family'.[104] Provision of benefit above subsistence level was an individual responsibility but it was the

State's responsibility to ensure that its measures 'leave room and encouragement for such voluntary insurance'.[105]

Beveridge reveals a significant element in his philosophy when he says that the principle of flat rate subsistence benefits 'follows from the recognition of the place and importance of voluntary insurance in social security'.[106] It is clearly his views about voluntary insurance which shape his ideas about the State scheme. He does not start from the idea of flat rate subsistence benefits and top up such a scheme by a voluntary addition. Rather he starts from the centrality of a voluntary element and underpins it with a State scheme. Voluntary insurance has two distinct roles — to provide benefits over and above the flat rate subsistence benefits of the State scheme and also to cover risks and needs which are common enough to be worth insuring against but not so uniform as to call for compulsory insurance.

Beveridge's plea was for the State to assume a comprehensive approach to social welfare — hence the way he based his plan for social insurance on three assumptions — a National Health Service, a scheme of Family Allowances and a policy of full employment. Removal of the economic barrier between patient and treatment was 'an essential negative step for bringing avoidable disease to an end', though positive steps to expand and develop preventive and curative facilities must follow.[107] He also made the obvious point that open access to medical care is a logical corollary of a State scheme for benefit during sickness. To let sickness continue for lack of treatment is an expense no government can afford. Family Allowances were a necessary element in any policy to secure a national minimum because the wages system on its own will not abolish poverty. A policy for full employment is required because simply to provide a subsistence income through insurance or assistance for those out of work is a totally inadequate provision for human happiness. The government should not feel that by making provision for income during unemployment it can avoid the prior responsibility of seeing that unemployment is reduced to a minimum.[108] Relief must be accompanied by treatment designed to cure the ills not simply to ease the pain.

The case which Beveridge argues for a wider State concern for welfare is not simply humanitarian. He also presses the argument that some welfare expenditure, for example on education, should be regarded as a communal investment, likely to bring a good return.[109] He argues the same investment case for Family Allowances. As regards unemployment benefit, he urges that provision on the most generous scale possible will help maintain purchasing power in depression, so mitigating its severity.[110]

Galbraith's attitude to the role of the State in welfare is pragmatic rather than ideological. He asserts the need for State responsibility, not as a matter of principle, but as a matter of necessity where other types of provision have failed. This is the burden of his argument for the New Socialism. He believes that an affluent society, by its very nature, increases the need for welfare intervention — for example, to care for the children whose mothers have returned to work so they can buy the goods which industry must produce and sell if full employment is to be maintained, or to combat the lawlessness to which affluent societies seem prone,[111] or to provide medical treatment for the health hazards generated by affluence — obesity, cirrhosis, accidents due to increased consumption of alcohol, lung cancer, heart disease, nervous diseases, and so on.[112]

Public intervention and provision develop because the very changes which increase the need for a wide range of welfare services, at the same time render their effective private provision less likely. The growth industries — the planning system — seize the ear of the State and become the prime beneficiaries of increased public spending. Public policy is geared to serving their needs — through higher education designed to produce the skills they require, through direct and indirect subsidies, public investment and markets for products, rather than ensuring the effective operation of health or housing services. The result is the contrast between the squalor of public services serving the needy but powerless and the affluence of services assisting the needy but powerful.

In Galbraith's view, the State's concern is with poverty rather than inequality, with social balance rather than redistribution. His proposals are often imaginative — for example, his proposal in 'The Affluent Society', long before positive discrimination became part of the conventional wisdom, that 'to eliminate poverty efficiently, we must, indeed, invest more than proportionately in the children of the poor community.'[113] His stress on achieving social balance rather than redistribution is an attempt to take welfare policy out of politics, to confine it to ills which all right-minded people recognise and deplore. Such a role is essentially limited.

The aim of the reluctant collectivists is to purge capitalism of its inefficiencies and its injustices so that it may survive. They believe that capitalism and planning are compatible, that government intervention is necessary to make capitalism morally acceptable. Their achievement has been to save capitalism and to preserve its essential elements while reducing or eliminating what had become unacceptable.

4

THE FAbiAN SociAlisTs

The socialist writers about the role of the State in welfare occupy a
substantial area of middle ground between the reluctant collectivists
and the Marxists. At the boundaries, the divisions between this group
and their neighbours are sometimes blurred. Trespassing is quite
frequent. There are, however, obvious differences. The socialist stress
on equality differentiates this group quite sharply from the reluctant
collectivists, so too does their more positive attitude to the possibilities
of government action. They differ from the Marxists on the other hand
in believing that capitalism can be transformed peacefully into
socialism.

Social values

There are three central socialist values — equality, freedom and
fellowship. We discuss in addition two other central but derivative
values — democracy, which is the child of equality and freedom, and
humanitarianism which is the offspring of equality and fellowship.
Sometimes there can be clashes between the values — for example
between equality and freedom or between humanitarianism and
freedom. Sometimes there is much more stress on one or two of these
values than on the others, but together they make up the basic value-
mix of British democratic socialism.

Equality, says Crosland, 'has been the strongest ethical inspiration of
virtually every socialist doctrine (and) still remains the most characteristic feature of socialist thought today.'[1] 'Where there is no egalitarianism,'

asserts Roy Jenkins, 'there is no socialism.'[2] For Tawney, equality was quite fundamental — 'the necessary corollary . . . of the Christian conception of man'.[3] The socialists argue the case for equality on four main grounds — social unity, social efficiency, social justice and individual self-realisation. In the sixty years spanned by the writings of Tawney and Crosland the arguments have remained remarkably similar.

In all his writings Tawney was deeply concerned about the problem of social integration. Writing in 1913, he spoke of a belief in equality as 'the one foundation of human subordination, of order, authority and justice'.[4] In the 1930s, he argued that the co-operation necessary to solve the country's economic ills was rendered impossible by the class struggle which had its roots in social and economic inequalities.[5] 'History suggests', Titmuss wrote, 'that human nature is not strong enough to maintain itself in true community where great disparities of income and wealth preside.'[6] Like Tawney, he saw a reduction of inequality as a necessary, but not a sufficient, condition of social harmony.

Crosland seeks to explain the continuing existence of 'so many touchy, prickly, indignant and frustrated citizens in politics and industry' by 'that resentment against social inequality which is characteristic of class antagonism'.[7] He explains this resentment in terms of society's failure to assimilate new economic groups who, as a result, find their social aspirations blocked. Such collective resentments 'feed on themselves, and become magnified and extended; and . . . threaten, in a way which purely random personal frustrations do not, other exceedingly important values — democracy, social and industrial peace, tolerance and even personal freedom.'[8]

The argument that inequality leads to inefficiency is based on two main grounds. First, massive inequalities lead to a misdirection of productive effort because the free market system responds to demand not to need. Pronounced inequalities will therefore lead to the production of cake for some before bread for all, of yachts and Rolls Royces before houses. Second, inequality is inefficient because it leads to a waste of ability.[9] 'If social mobility is low,' Crosland writes, 'as it must be in a stratified society, and people cannot easily move up from the lower or middle reaches to the top, then the ruling elite becomes hereditary and self-perpetuating; and whatever one may concede to inherited or family advantages, this must involve a waste of talent.'[10]

There are three main reasons why social inequalities offend against ideas of social justice. First, they lead to a denial of natural rights. 'The solid rock at the core of the argument for equality', says Douglas Jay, '. . . must remain the equal moral claim of all men to basic human rights.'[11] Such rights are denied when, for example, educational opportunities are distributed, not according to ability but according to the accidents of birth and parental income. Crosland makes explicit the denial of justice which this involves. Every child, he argues, has a natural 'right' as a citizen 'not merely to "life, liberty and the pursuit of happiness" but to that position in the social scale to which his natural talents entitle him.'[12] Inequality of opportunity in education frustrates this natural right.

Second, inequality is unjust because it is the product of a system of rewards and privileges which is indefensible because unprincipled. It endows a minority lavishly because of the accidents of birth or inheritance rather than according to contribution to the common good.

Third, inequalities offend against ideas of justice because they give certain groups immense power over others. No one, Crosland argues, whether landlord, employer or manager 'has any obvious moral right' to the untrammelled power to which social inequality contributes.[13] Tawney returns again and again to the injustice of a system which treats men as 'hands' rather than men. The basis of such a system is inequality of power.

The final argument for equality is that it is only in a more equal society that the individual has the opportunity to realise his potentialities. A society is civilised, Tawney argued, in so far as it uses its material resources to provide for the dignity and refinement of the individual human beings who compose it. 'Violent contrasts of wealth and power, and an undiscriminating devotion to institutions by which such contrasts are maintained and heightened, do not promote the attainment of such ends but thwart it.'[14] Man's basic humanity is thus diminished by inequality.

For the socialist equality means more than a simple equality of opportunity. Forty years ago Tawney argued that the essential weakness of the idea of equality of opportunity was that too often it has been presented in negative rather than positive terms. 'It has been interpreted rather as freedom from restraints than as the possession of powers. Thus conceived, it has at once the grandeur and unreality of a majestic phantom.'[15] The existence of equality of opportunity, he continued, 'depends not merely on the absence of disabilities, but on the presence of abilities . . . In proportion, as the capacities of some are sterilised or stunted by their social environment, while those of others are favoured or pampered by it, equality of opportunity becomes a graceful, but attenuated, figment.'[16] For Tawney, therefore, if equality of opportunity is to be real, it must be preceded and accompanied by equalising measures.

Tawney and Crosland agree that, in other ways, the limited goal of equality of opportunity 'is not, from a socialist point of view, sufficient.'[17] Individual happiness, says Tawney, requires not only that men should be able to rise but that they should be able to live a life of dignity and culture whether they rise or not.[18] So it is not enough simply to place a director's brief case in every worker's knapsack. Crosland extends this point, emphasising that if the present inequality of rewards continues to exist alongside greater equality of opportunity, many of the discontents associated with equality of opportunity will inevitably survive. Indeed, they may get worse because 'if the inequality of rewards is excessively great, the creation of equal opportunities may give rise to too intense a competition, with a real danger of increased frustration and discontent.'[19]

To the socialist, 'equality ' means more than equality of opportunity but less than equality of income. Equality of incomes is not advocated for three main reasons. First, says Tawney, 'No one thinks it inequitable that, when a reasonable provision has been made for all, exceptional responsibilities should be compensated by exceptional rewards, as a recognition of the service performed and an inducement to perform it.'[20] Crosland suggests the second reason in his statement that 'extra responsibility and exceptional talent require and deserve a differential reward '[21] — the implication being that inequalities are necessary to mobilise skills. The third reason is that the preservation of equality of incomes would require such regulation that it could not be maintained in a free society.[22]

It is in relation to income distribution that Crosland emerges most clearly as a meritocratic egalitarian. What is fundamentally unjust about the present pattern of income distribution, in his view, is the absence of an equal opportunity of attaining the top rewards. 'The essential thing', he writes, 'is that every citizen should have an equal chance — that is his basic democratic right; but provided the start is fair, let there be the maximum scope for individual self-advancement. There would then be nothing improper in either a high continuous status ladder (e.g. of income or consumption patterns) or even a distinct class stratification (e.g. a segregated educational system), since opportunities for attaining the highest status or the topmost stratum would be genuinely equal.'[23] In Crosland's most recent statement of the essentials of Labour policy for the 1970s, action on equality of income does not secure a mention.[24]

While the socialist interpretation of equality does not mean that all incomes should be equal, it does demand a move towards a more equal distribution of wealth because the existing distribution is 'flagrantly unjust'.[25] Crosland does not, however, condemn inequalities of wealth in principle. It is their origins which make them acceptable or unacceptable. In his view, inequalities of wealth may be considered unjust for three reasons — if they stem from inherited property and not from work, if they reflect differences in opportunity rather than differences in ability, and if they are the product of unequally generous treatment by the tax system.[26] It is against inequalities deriving from inherited wealth that socialists have directed their fiercest criticisms. Given the current distribution of wealth, said Tawney, 'inheritance is on the way to becoming little more than a device by which a small minority of rich men bequeath to their heirs a right to free quarters at the expense of their fellow countrymen.'[27]

Crosland brushes aside the question of how much equality is desirable. The practising politician is not, he believes, required to answer this difficult question. His task is rather to tackle existing glaring and obviously dysfunctional inequalities — in particular those which are in no sense the product of individual effort, which are wholly irrelevant to economic growth and which are offensive to ideas of social justice. The relationship between equality and incentives and equality and fairness can safely be left to others.[28] Crosland is nevertheless quite explicit that 'a definite limit exists to the degree of equality which is desirable.'[29]

Three elements in particular distinguish the socialist conception of freedom. First, the socialist holds that a belief in freedom means, as a necessary corollary, a concern for equality. Freedom rests on equality because if there are major inequalities of resources or power some men are in bondage to others. The fundamental idea of liberty, says Tawney, is power to control the condition of one's own life — and this means equality.[30]

Second, the socialist seeks to extend the idea of freedom from the political to the economic sphere. Economic freedom means that men should have a voice in the conditions of their work, that they should be recognised as possessing certain rights in relation to it, that no one should be in a position to exercise arbitrary power of regulation or dismissal over them.[31]

Third, the socialist believes that freedom is the product of government action rather than government inaction. Only government action through law, economic, social and fiscal policy can redistribute freedom so that its exercise can become a reality for all. 'The increase in the freedom of ordinary men and women during the last two generations', Tawney wrote in 1949, 'has taken place, not in spite of the action of governments, but because of it . . . The mother of liberty has, in fact, been law.'[32]

'The socialist system of values included a distinctive view of equality and liberty', writes Samuel Beer, 'but one gets at the heart of its ethical message with the concept of fellowship.'[33] By fellowship, the socialist means co-operation rather than competition, an emphasis on duties rather than on rights, on the good of the community rather than on the wants of the individual, on altruism rather than on self-help.

The basis of Tawney's critique of the acquisitive society is the way in which it invites men to use the powers and skills, with which they have been endowed, for their own profit rather than for the good of society. The acquisitive society, he wrote, 'makes the individual the centre of his own universe.'[34] In his view, 'The individual has no absolute rights; they are relative to the function which he performs in the community of which he is a member.'[35] Rights are conditional and derivative. Their source is the ends and purposes of society. If society is to be healthy, men must regard themselves 'not primarily as the owners of rights, but as trustees for the discharge of functions and the instruments of a social purpose'.[36] For Tawney the essence of socialism was 'the substitution of the ideal of service for that of getting on'.[37]

In his list of the basic socialist aspirations Crosland puts in fourth place 'a rejection of competitive antagonism, and an ideal of fraternity and co-operation'.[38] Titmuss is equally emphatic when he writes that 'socialism is about community as well as equality.'[39] The importance of altruism and giving to strangers is, of course, the central theme of 'The Gift Relationship'. 'There is nothing permanent', Titmuss writes, 'about the expression of reciprocity. If the bonds of community giving are broken the result is not a state of value neutralism. The vacuum is likely to be filled by hostility and social conflict.'[40] Altruism and a sense of concern and responsibility for others and for the community as a whole were, in his view, essential to peaceful and healthy society.

The socialist emphasis on democracy and participation is the product of a belief in equality and a conviction that a man should have a say in issues which affect him. 'Democracy', says Tawney, 'in one form or another is not merely one of several alternative methods of establishing a socialist commonwealth. It is an essential condition of such a commonwealth's existence.'[41] Durbin made the same point insisting that 'the democratic method is an inherent part of socialism.'[42]

Socialists, however, regard political democracy as only one element in a truly democratic society. The essence of socialism is 'the extension of democratic principles into spheres of life which previously escaped their influence.' 'It is impossible', Cole argued, 'to have a really democratic society if most of the members have to spend most of their lives at work under essentially undemocratic conditions . . . Industrial democracy is, therefore, an indispensable part of social democracy, that is of socialism.'[43]

Crosland argues that the same kind of case for more democracy and participation applies in the management of local authority housing estates. 'We must seek to give him (the Council tenant) a security, an independence and a freedom to do what he likes in his house, which is comparable to that of the owner occupier. A programme for greater tenants' democracy should, therefore, form a central, and probably the most novel, part of a Labour housing programme.'[44]

The arguments for more participation are practical as well as idealistic. As Tawney pointed out,[45]

It is idle to expect that men will give their best to any system which they do not trust, or that they will trust any system in the control of which they do not share . . . The Public cannot have it both ways. If it allows workmen to be treated as 'hands', it cannot claim the service of their wills and their brains. If it desires them to show the zeal of skilled professionals, it must secure that they have sufficient power to allow of their discharging professional responsibilities.

Titmuss expresses his democratic values in his stress on the need to curb sources of economic and social power which are responsible to no one. He emphasises the consequences which flow from the power of great financial institutions like insurance companies and building societies. 'Social policies will be imposed without democratic discussion; without consideration of the moral consequences which may result from them. In this sense they will be irresponsible decisions.'[46] Such institutions are concerned with no social objectives, simply with safeguarding the interests of their policy or shareholders.[47] To a democratic socialist, such arbitrary and private power challenges fundamental values.

Another central socialist value is humanitarianism, a deep concern that people should be able to fulfil what they have it within them to become and that social distress should be swept away. Why, Tawney asks, do we condemn certain kinds of activity — he instances sweating — which are convenient to the majority and contribute to the greatest good of the greatest number. His answer is that no amount of convenience or benefit to the majority can justify any injustice to the minority, 'Because the personality of man is the most divine thing we know and to encroach upon it is to efface the very title deeds of humanity.'[48] Tawney's fundamental criticism of capitalism is that it treats men 'not as human personalities, but as tools, not as ends but as means.'[49]

Crosland sees this practical non-doctrinal humanitarian attack on social distress as 'much the most powerful inspiration from the earliest days of the Labour Party'.[50] He emphasises that it is humanitarianism not egalitarianism which underlies the socialist's concern for the relief of distress and the elimination of squalor. To the socialist living in the affluence of contemporary Britain, 'the uncivilised state of the social sector, so deadening to happiness and vitality' stands out as 'unendurable'.[51]

Because of his concern with welfare the socialist will give an exceptionally high priority to traditional social welfare goals[52] and to the devotion of an increased proportion of the national income to social purposes.

Titmuss's humanitarianism emerges in his definition of 'social growth'. This, he believes, should be our priority rather than economic growth. Social growth means spending proportionately more on the educationally deprived than on the educationally normal, pressing forward with the rehousing of the poor more rapidly than with the rehousing of the better off and devoting proportionately more medical care to the needs of the chronic sick than to those of the average sick.[53]

Society and the State

The socialists differ quite considerably from each other in how they see society. At one extreme, there are those who adopt a near Marxist analysis and reject root and branch the capitalist system and the patterns of economic and social relations which go with it. At the other extreme, there are those revisionists who would find comparatively little to divide them from the reluctant collectivists, and who see the ills of capitalism as requiring correction rather than the rejection of the system as a whole.

If we look first at the economic structure, these differences emerge quite sharply in the socialist analysis of capitalism. The fundamentalists see the eradication of capitalism and the widespread extension of public ownership as necessary to achieve their aims. The revisionists would accept that such action might once have been necessary or desirable but argue that the need for it has passed. 'By 1951', Crosland asserts, 'Britain had, in all the essentials, ceased to be a capitalist country.'[54] The political authority has emerged 'as the final arbiter of economic life', the classical entrepreneur has largely disappeared, the ownership of private industrial capital has become much less important, the ideology of capitalism has changed, intense class antagonisms have faded.[55]

The revisionist believes that this new capitalism can be tamed and harnessed to socialist aims, that the market system duly controlled, modified, supplemented, partially and temporarily superseded, can be made acceptable. The mixed economy becomes the end of a journey rather than a staging post. Competition and incentives, profits and entrepreneurial skills become legitimate. Our thesis, Crosland writes, reviewing the revisionist position, was that the ownership of the means of production was no longer the key factor which imparted to society its essential character. 'Collectivism, private ownership or a mixed economy were all consistent with widely varying degrees not only of equality, but also of freedom, democracy, exploitation, class feeling, elitism, industrial democracy, planning and economic growth. It was, therefore, possible to achieve the goal of greater equality and other desirable ends within the framework of a mixed economy, with public ownership taking its place as only one of a number of possible means for attaining the ends in view.'[56] Such an approach is a far cry from

Tawney's eloquent indictments of the very nature of capitalism.[57]

These differing diagnoses of the state of capitalism lead to fundamentally different attitudes to public ownership. The revisionist sees the separation of ownership from control as one of the key aspects of the new capitalism. If ownership and control are indeed separable, then the State in its turn does not need to assume ownership to enforce its will. And if the ownership of the means of production is not the factor which imparts to a society its essential character, then a change of ownership is not going to make vast differences. Public ownership is no longer seen as the essential prelude to the inauguration of the new society but rather as, in Jay's words, 'a means to social justice and only one means at that'.[58] The traditional view — epitomised for example by Tawney and Durbin — saw the extension of public ownership not as an end in itself but as vitally necessary to the general achievement of socialist objectives. The revisionist view is that public ownership is to be used pragmatically and selectively for the achievement of specific objectives.

In spite of their differing analyses of capitalism the socialists show a high level of agreement in the criticisms they make of the free market system. Their charges can be grouped under five headings.

The first one represents the main burden of Tawney's attack on acquisitive societies. It is that 'the motive which gives colour and quality to their public institutions, to their policy and political thought, is not the attempt to secure the fulfilment of tasks undertaken for the public service but to increase the opportunities open to individuals of attaining the objects which they conceive to be advantageous to themselves.'[59] It is a system which excludes consideration of collective goals because the only acceptable collective goal is that individuals should be free to pursue their own interests. In such a society there can be no clear social purpose. The result is at best an uneven pattern of public services, at worst, avoidable ills and public squalor.

The second charge is that the market system is undemocratic. Decisions important to many individuals are taken either in the gilded privacy of the corridors of power to which the majority have no access, or are not taken at all, but left to the capricious whim of market forces. It is on the first ground that Titmuss, as we pointed out earlier, indicts the private insurance companies 'because they constitute a major shift in economic power in our society. It is a power, a potential power, to affect many important aspects of our economic life and our social values . . . It is power concentrated in relatively few hands, working at the apex of a handful of giant bureaucracies, technically supported by a group of professional experts, and accountable, in practice, to virtually no one.'[60]

Third, the market system is unjust. The rewards it distributes are based on no clear principles and the lack of principle is inevitable in a society where each individual has a prescriptive moral right to what he can extract from his fellow citizens without contravening the law.[61] Crosland makes a rather different criticism of the injustice of the market systems when he criticises the injustice of a society which does not offer its members an equal chance of attaining the highest rewards.[62] The free market system is unjust too because it allows the costs of economic and social change — the diswelfares inherent in economic and social development — to lie where they fall.

A fourth charge in which the socialists join the reluctant collectivists is that the free market system is not self-regulating but rather is inefficient unless regulated positively by government.

The fifth and final charge is that the free market system has not abolished, will not, and cannot abolish poverty let alone inequality. None of the evidence for Britain or the United States over the last twenty years, Titmuss argues, supports the assumption that economic growth on its own can solve the problem of poverty.[63] Crosland sees the natural tendency of unregulated capitalism as being towards a cumulative increase in inequality.[64]

As regards the social structure the socialists all stress the divisions in society, most obviously between those who direct and own the material apparatus of industry and those who perform its routine work. Such divisions are inherent in the nature of an acquisitive capitalist society because they have their roots in functionless property. The result is a class struggle — obvious, regrettable but permanent in this kind of society. The struggle is not simply about rewards. It is wider than that and embraces 'the claims of common men to live their lives on the plane which a century of scientific progress has now made possible and the reluctance of property to surrender its special privileges'.[65] The underlying reason for this conflict, in Tawney's view, is the absence of social purpose.[66]

Crosland too stresses the survival of 'a disturbing amount . . . of social antagonism and class resentment, visible both in politics and industry'.[67] He accepts as inevitable the divergence of class interests and the conflict actual or potential between the two sides of industry. His most recent judgment is that 'an amazing sense of class' still survives and that 'Class relations in industry are characterised by a mutual distrust amounting often to open warfare.'[68] Titmuss stresses not class conflict but rather conflict between interest groups in society and speaks of 'the growth of a "Pressure Group State", generated by more massive concentrations of interlocking economic, managerial and self-regarding professional power'.[69]

As regards the political structure the socialists differ over the location of power. It is the owners of property who, in Tawney's view, dictate the character, development and organisation of society.[70] It is because of the key importance of economic power in determining political power that its transference to public hands is such a high priority. Tawney was confident, however, that the centres of economic power would 'probably yield, though only after two elections, to an overwhelming demonstration of opinion, in which the public shows its teeth'.[71]

Crosland's analysis differs fundamentally from Tawney's and even allowing for the twenty-five years separating their work, it is difficult to believe that they are compatible. In Crosland's view, capitalism has been transformed and there is today no capitalist ruling class. Power has passed to the political authority. In his view, economic power poses fewer problems today than other forms of power such as the power of the bureaucracy and the power of the media.[72]

Even with these differing views of the strength and significance of economic power, the socialists share a common view of the State. The State, said Tawney, is an instrument. 'Fools will use it, when they can, for foolish ends, criminals for criminal ends. Sensible and decent men will use it for ends which are sensible and decent. We, in England, have repeatedly remade the state, and we are remaking it now, and shall remake it again.'[73] Crosland dismisses out of hand the Marxist view of the State as the executive committee of the capitalist class. His thesis is that today economic power belongs to the owners of political power, and that a determined government can generally successfully impose its will on private industry.[74]

The socialists believe, therefore, that united social action is possible — hence their faith in government. 'Society is not an economic mechanism', Tawney wrote, 'but a community of wills which are often discordant, but which are capable of being inspired by devotion to common ends.'[75]

The role of government

Given his five central values and his view of society, how does the socialist hope to see his hopes realised? The answer is that he looks to purposeful government action. Some socialists are still troubled by the strength of countervailing economic power responsible to no public authority. Others have their doubts about the ability of the Labour Party to be an instrument of radical social change. But there is little general questioning of the ability of government to enforce its will and achieve its aims. Looking back in sorrow rather than in anger at the limited Labour achievements both in opposition and between 1964 and 1970, Crosland's recipe for greater success is 'a sharper delineation of fundamental objectives, a greater clarity about egalitarian priorities and a stronger determination to achieve them'.[76] Labour's failures, in his view, were seen as the result of its own weaknesses rather than the strength of the forces opposing it.

The socialist's view of the role of government follows from his analysis of the failings of the free market system. Essentially, the task of government is to correct, supplement and supplant the market system in the interests of equality, freedom, fellowship, democracy and welfare. First of all, as we have seen, the socialist sees the market system as being concerned primarily with individual rights rather than social purposes. Because of this it is essentially an undemocratic system. The socialist argues that it is a responsibility of government to ensure that industry operates in the light of social need rather than private self-interest. The fundamental case for public ownership, in Tawney's view, was that private ownership diverts industry 'from the performance of function to the acquisition of gain'.[77] Crosland, fifty years later, is equally clear about the duty of government — though less certain about methods. 'It is the direct responsibility of the democratic state, as guardian of the public welfare', he writes, 'to lay down the detailed ground rules and compel the private (and the nationalised) firm to conform to its own positive views of where the public interest lies.'[78]

Another aspect of this criticism that the free market system lacks a clear social purpose is the charge that it is inefficient at achieving communal purposes. It is concerned and able to weigh only private costs. One of the duties of government, as the socialist sees it, is to weigh general social costs and benefits and make decisions on this basis. 'Politics', Tawney wrote, 'are, or ought to be, the art of achieving by collective action those ends which individuals cannot achieve, or cannot achieve with the same measure of success, by their isolated efforts.'[79]

The socialist sees it as a task of government to modify what he sees as the injustices of the market system of distribution. His concern for welfare and equality lead to a certain view of collective responsibility. This, says Crosland, 'represents the first major difference between a socialist and a conservative.'[80] He explains that the difference is 'not because Conservatives are necessarily less humanitarian, but because they hold particular views as to the proper role of the state, the desirable level of taxation and the importance of private as opposed to collective responsibility. Their willingness for social expenditure is circumscribed by these views and the consequence is a quite different order of priorities.'[81]

For the socialist, a just society requires distribution not simply according to market power. A distribution according to the arbitrary criteria of market forces, and a passive acceptance that the costs of economic and social change should lie where they fall, are anathema to the socialist. He sees the individual and communal diswelfares resulting from economic and social development as a charge that should be assumed by the community as a whole and shared as equitably as possible among its members.

The socialist will also be concerned to use the power of government to modify the market distribution of power and freedom. In opposition to the belief that planning is the road to serfdom he believes that 'it is as possible to plan for freedom as for tyranny.'[82] He believes too that, if 'freedom implies, as presumably it does, the possession by individuals of a genuine, if partial, power of self determination, then, so far from having been attenuated by measures conducive to the more general enjoyment of physical and mental vitality, it has gained in substance and reality as a result of them.'[83] Crosland argues for the municipalisation of private rented housing on grounds of power and freedom. 'Private landlordism', he insists, 'is not an appropriate form of house ownership in an advanced society. The relationship between landlord and tenant is too unequal; and the landlord wields a degree of power over his tenant's life which is unacceptable in a democratic society.'[84]

In the view of the revisionists, it is a crucial responsibility of government to secure economic growth. Tawney argued that the problem of distribution was one not of amounts but of proportions. More recently Crosland has argued that socialist goals are unattainable without economic growth.[85] Redistribution of the national income from private consumption to social expenditure in a democracy is only possible, he believes, when total resources are growing rapidly. Growth is also important to socialists because it enlarges personal freedom by giving people more choice, because it increases the subjective sense of equality by reducing the more obvious disparities between rich and poor, and because it is the only way to tackle the replacement of our outworn social capital. Given a rapidly growing economy the government must work to counteract the tendencies towards a cumulative increase in inequality inherent in such growth, through action such as the public ownership of land, the taxation of capital gains, a wealth tax, a gifts tax and a prices and incomes policy.[86]

The welfare state

The socialist's attitude towards the welfare state is one of enthusiastic approval and support. The Fabians believed that through gradualism and permeation the capitalist state could be persuaded to reform itself. The welfare state is the fruit of this approach. Crosland describes the welfare state tradition as 'perhaps the most deeply felt item in Labour policy'.[87] In setting out what Labour stands for in the 1970s, he puts first 'an exceptionally high priority, when considering the claims on our resources, for the relief of poverty, distress and social squalor — Labour's traditional "social welfare" goal.'[88]

Increased social spending has generally been approved by socialists. There have been critics from the left who describe the services as 'mere palliatives' and there have been critics from the right arguing against generalised social expenditure as the answer to all social ills, but both these groups have been very much in a minority. The strength of the pragmatic, piecemeal social engineering, Fabian tradition has led to the acceptance of welfare statism as the key element in Labour policy. Whether the welfare state was to be regarded as the realisation of the socialist dream or merely as a staging point on the journey to the new society has troubled some thinkers, but such theorising has been foreign to the unspeculative, empirical tradition of British socialism.

Socialist attitudes towards the welfare state have been essentially pragmatic. It has been interpreted as a logical response to practical problems, as the product of the impact of industrialisation, urbanisation, technological change and democracy. 'The causes of the movement', Tawney wrote, 'are not obscure. It is the natural consequence of the simultaneous development of an industrial civilisation and of political democracy.'[89] T.H. Marshall's discussion of the evolution of ideas of social rights as the main element in the development of social policy and his conclusion that the basis of the British welfare state 'belongs to democracy more than to Socialism',[90] would be widely accepted by socialists.

Speaking of the social policy measures which came into effect in 1948, Titmuss disassociates himself from those 'who thought that these policy changes were brought about for deliberately redistributive reasons or that the effects would be significantly egalitarian'. In his view, 'the fundamental and dominating historical processes which led to these major changes in social policy were connected with the demand for one society.'[91]

In his most recent writings Crosland also uses this citizenship-democracy model. 'I believe', he says speaking of the movement towards comprehensive education, 'this represents a strong and irresistible pressure on British society to extend the rights of citizenship. Over the past 300 years these rights have been extended first to personal liberty then to political democracy, and later to social welfare. Now they must be further extended to educational equality.'[92]

The socialist response to those who criticise the welfare state for the burden it imposes on public expenditure, or for the way it restricts choice and freedom, is to stress its important social and economic functions and to emphasise social policy as a pragmatic response to the problems and needs of industrial society. Such a response serves both as explanation and justification.

There is much emphasis in socialist writings about the welfare state on the contribution of social expenditure to economic growth. Expenditure on education and health, it is argued, should be seen as investment rather than as consumption. Wage related unemployment benefits and redundancy payments should be seen as a positive attempt to grease the wheels of technological and industrial change.

'It is one of the major functions of social security and social service programmes', Titmuss has argued, 'to make some provision for these victims of diswelfare; to compensate them in part for income loss or other injuries to life chances.'[93] As Titmuss points out elsewhere, 'Every factor contributing to economic growth is also a factor contributing to social need.'[94]

Equally, there is stress on the social functions of welfare provision. Titmuss, for example, emphasises that many social services should be seen as a response to changes in the roles and functions of the family. 'It is in this context', he writes, 'that we need to see the social services in a variety of stabilising, preventive and protective roles. Interpreted in this way and not as the modern equivalent of Bismarkian benevolence, the social services become an ally — not an enemy of industrial and technological progress.'[95]

Titmuss also stresses the functions of social policy in maintaining social integration, a sense of community and a sense of altruism — all of which he sees as crucial to social health and well being. In Titmuss's view, the National Health Service 'has allowed and encouraged sentiments of altruism, reciprocity and social duty to express themselves.' He goes on to argue that 'the ways in which society organises and structures its social institutions — and particularly its health and welfare systems — can encourage or discourage the altruistic in man; such systems can foster integration or alienation.'[96] Because giving is a crucial element in a healthy society, the case for social rather than economic markets in certain areas of life takes on a new importance.

Socialists also emphasise the humanitarian aims and purposes of the welfare state, as against its concern with equality. 'Social equality', says Crosland, 'cannot be held to be the ultimate purpose of the social services. This must surely be the relief of social distress and hardship and the correction of social need; though naturally measures directed to this end will often also enhance social equality, which in any case remains an important subsidiary objective.'[97]

Marshall argues along the same lines. Of the three types of aim which social policy can have — the elimination of poverty, the maximisation of welfare and the pursuit of equality — the second, in his view, 'expresses the philosophy of the welfare state.'[98] 'The extension of the social services', he thinks, 'is not primarily a means of equalizing incomes ... What matters is that there is a general enrichment of the concrete substance of civilized life, a general reduction of risk and insecurity.'[99] Crosland's humanitarian-welfare focus comes out clearly in his discussion of the needs of special groups. 'To accord these special problems an overriding priority', he argues, 'should be a characteristic, even more than a belief in equality, of a socialist outlook.'[100]

Early writers such as Tawney stressed the redistributive possibilities of communal expenditure. What excited Tawney was not the magnitude of the redistribution effected by the social services, but rather the magnitude of the results which even a slender and reluctant measure of redistribution could produce. Through the pooling of its resources a society could abolish 'the most crushing of the disabilities and the most odious of the privileges which drive a chasm across it. It can generalise, by collective action, advantages associated in the past with the owner-ship of property ... it can secure that, in addition to the payments made to them for their labour, its citizens enjoy a social income which ... is available on equal terms to all its members.'[101]

Socialists see the welfare state as being concerned with the various types of redistribution necessary and desirable in a complex society. Economic growth requires the redistribution of educational oppor-tunity through free education. Individual and social well-being require various types of redistribution of income over the life cycle from the young to the old, from the employed to the unemployed, from the healthy to the sick, from people without children to families with children. The concern, as Crosland suggests, is with welfare rather than equality, with compensation to temper the chill winds of market forces rather than with vertical redistribution on egalitarian grounds. He welcomes this idea of social income for basic needs but an extension of the principle would, in his view, soon become an interference with individual freedom. 'It is not a part of socialism', he concludes, 'continually to tell people how to spend their incomes.'[102]

Crosland's views on the socialist attitude to private provision are typical of many. In essence, his answer is to leave the private sector alone and to strive to make the public sector so good that there is no qualitative difference between the two.[103] He rejects, for example, the idea of simply closing down the public schools as out of tune with the temper of the country and because 'the interference with private liberty would be intolerable.'[104] 'The object', he argues, 'would be not to prohibit all private fee paying ... but by regulating the conditions under which education is bought and sold, to secure a more equitable distribution of educational resources between different classes.'[105]

Titmuss makes the most detailed and important analysis of the effects of private provision. 'Until we, as a society', he argues, 'can rid ourselves of the dominating influence of the private sector of education, we shall not have the will to embark on an immensely higher standard of provision for all those children whose education now finishes when it has hardly begun.'[106] He argues the same point in relation to occupational welfare provision. As such private services expand and proliferate, 'they come into conflict with the aims and unity of social policy; for in effect (whatever their aims may be) their whole tendency at present is to divide loyalties, to nourish privilege and to narrow the social conscience.'[107] Those who are provided for privately are less concerned about the general level of social provision. Indeed 'one of the functions of the atomistic private market system is to "free" men from any sense of obligation to and for other men.'[108]

The benefits provided privately are at levels far higher than can be attained by public provision. As a result, 'it is possible to see two nations in old age; greater inequalities in living standards after work than in work; two contrasting social services for distinct groups based on different principles and operating in isolation of each other.'[109] Another strand in Titmuss's argument is that private provision in fact narrows and restricts freedom rather than extends it. 'For the mass of the population included in private schemes there is virtually no choice, no reality or sense of democratic participation and few if any formal channels for redress of wrongs.'[110]

A major element in Titmuss's thinking about the role of social policy is his stress on its force as an instrument for social integration. Private welfare institutions such as insurance companies and building societies, have no such concern and their policies can work in exactly the opposite direction. Through their rejection of certain 'bad risk' minority groups they can contribute to a sense of powerlessness and alienation.[111]

Titmuss is critical of private provision, too, for the immense power it places in the hands of key financial institutions and their anonymous technocrats. Their investment decisions could be of major importance for the restoration of the outworn, mid-Victorian social capital of social considerations but there is, in fact, little or no public discussion of the choices available, of the common good, or of the implications of the decisions that are made.[112]

T.H. Marshall sees the correct balance between public and private welfare provision as crucial to the stability of the democratic-welfare-capitalist society that has evolved in Britain. If contracting out of public services like health and education were allowed on a large scale, 'A point would soon be reached at which the whole conception of a community dedicated to providing for the vital needs of its members by systems of mutual aid would be lost, and the balance between the elements constituting the democratic-welfare-capitalist society destroyed.'[113]

Titmuss argues that the principles of universality as applied to the main social services in 1948 'was needed as a major objective favouring social integration; as a method of breaking down distinctions and discriminative tests between first and second-class citizens.'[114] Very soon, however, this principle of universal free availability began to be questioned. Crosland argued in 1956 that while social equality required universal availability of services, it did not always require universal free availability. He emphasised the difference between a test of means which determines the right to use a service and one which simply determines the question of payment. In his view, an income test to determine whether access to the service should or should not be free was quite acceptable provided that two conditions were fulfilled. 'First, the benefit or services must not be so essential, and so large in relation to the recipient's means, that he may reasonably consider he has a social right to it, so that both his real income and self-esteem would be severely affected by a test of means. This rules out an income test for the basic cash benefits, which often constitute almost the whole of the recipient's income, and for the central, essential health and education services. Secondly, the income-line should be set as high as possible. If only paupers are excluded from the need to pay, there is more danger of inferior feeling arising than if only surtax payers are compelled to pay.' Of itself, Crosland argued, universality cannot create social equality; attainment of equality depends less on free universality than on 'the creation of standards of public health, education and housing so high that no marked qualitative gap remains between public and private provision. It will then matter little whether or not occasional charges are imposed, subject to the above conditions.'[115]

In addition to the point that free, universal services cannot of themselves create equality, Crosland makes two other important points. First he argues that 'the traditional means of universal, indiscriminate social services are . . . not always the most appropriate to the more subtle social problems which remain.'[116] Second, he argues that 'we cannot afford to spread social expenditure thinly over needy and nonneedy alike, but must concentrate it heavily on those points where the need is greatest.'[117] Socialists have tended to take up and develop this first point, Conservatives the second.

The socialist critique of universalism has had two essential elements — first that the main beneficiaries of the high cost areas of social welfare have been the middle classes — 'the more that is spent on higher education the more the poor are subsidising the rich, who benefit most from it.'[118] The second element in the critique is the conclusion that universalism on its own does not solve the problem of conveying services to the poor and hard to reach. Universalism is essential but it is only a start. 'The challenge that faces us', according to Titmuss, 'is not the choice between universalist and selective services. The real challenge resides in the question: what particular infrastructure of universalist services is needed in order to provide a framework of values and opportunity bases within and around which can be developed acceptable selective services provided, as social rights, on criteria of needs of specific categories, groups and territorial areas and not dependent on individual tests of means?'[119] What Titmuss wants is positive discrimination, egalitarian selectivity.

In general, socialists are opposed to means tested welfare benefits both on practical and fundamental grounds. They oppose them on the simple practical ground that they fail to achieve their object since people do not apply either for reasons of ignorance or because they dislike the implications of a means tested system. Socialists also dislike means tested benefits because their ultimate aim is to restrict demand rather than to meet need, because of the sense of stigma which they can impose, because of the idea they proclaim that the needy are a burden, because of the way they offend against ideas of social equality by isolating the most needy and reducing them to the status of applicants or suppliants, and because they imply that the social services exist only for the needy and that social expenditure should always, as a matter of principle, be reduced to the lowest possible level.

While supporting the aims and purposes of the welfare state, socialists have remained aware of its limitations and its dangers. They voice four general fears — that it is concerned with injustice rather than with justice, that it can be used by government as a substitute for necessary preventive action, that it can be limited to seeking equality of opportunity, that it is concerned with poverty not with inequality.

In the very early days of State welfare provision, Tawney pointed out the danger implicit in the social reformers' preoccupation with the exceptional misfortunes of life at the expense of an extension of the opportunity for the majority to live a life of security and independence.[120] Titmuss makes a rather similar point looking at the achievements of State welfare twenty years after 1948. In his judgment, 'Thought, research and action have been focused too heavily on the poor; poverty engineering has thus been abstracted from society. Social policy has been seen as an ad hoc appendage to economic growth, the provision of benefits, not the formulation of rights.'[121]

Tawney also saw the danger that social provision can be used by the State 'as a lazy substitute for the attempt to prevent the contingency from occurring'. The limit to the extension of social provision, he wrote, is obvious. 'It is drawn at the point where measures to protect the individual from being crushed by a contingency, when it occurs, become liable to be used by the state as a lazy substitute for the attempt to prevent the contingency from occurring.'[122]

Tawney criticised too the notion of equality of opportunity as the answer to the problem of inequality. He refused to countenance the argument that 'the presence of opportunities, by which individuals can ascend and get on, relieves economic contrasts of their social poison and their personal sting.' Such an attitude towards social inequality he found quite unacceptable. Furthermore, he rejected the idea that equality of opportunity could ever be attained in a society where people's circumstances were so unequal from the moment of birth.[123]

Another criticism which Tawney makes is that the traditional measures which we have come to subsume under the term the welfare state — State regulation, the policy of the national minimum etc., increase the well being of the classes who are protected. 'But it does not touch the problem of inequality based on economic privilege, which is, I think, even more than poverty, the great blot on modern society.'[124]

Many commentators have made the point that whatever else it has achieved, the advent of the 'welfare state' in Britain after the second world war has not led to any significant redistribution of wealth, income or opportunity. A factor which Titmuss emphasises is that government and people alike were mesmerised by the language of the welfare state. 'It was assumed too readily after 1948', he writes, 'that all the answers had been found to the problems of health, education, social welfare and housing and that what was little more than an administrative tidying up of social security provisions represented a social revolution.'[125] So much was spoken and written about the abolition of poverty, and the arrival of equality of opportunity that people assumed they had come to pass. It was assumed that legislation led to provision, and to provision which was equally accessible to all. There was a failure to grasp the complexity of the problems of deprivation and to appreciate the difficulties of reaching poor and minority groups and of getting them to use universal services.[126]

Another element in the failure, which Titmuss mentions, is the lack of tools to monitor the effects of social change and the overall impact of an expansion of public and private welfare services. Given this lack of tools, and so of evidence, the belief that growing affluence had solved, or would soon solve, all our major problems reigned supreme.[127]

Crosland suggests two further explanations. There has, he thinks, been a lack of clarity about objectives. Social expenditure has been ineffective in reducing poverty and inequality because these have not been set out or accepted as explicit aims. Because of this, there has been too little attempt to co-ordinate policies, particularly in deprived inner urban areas.[128] For Crosland, however, the most important explanation for the limited success of the welfare state is the failure of successive governments to achieve economic growth. In his frequently reiterated view, further redistribution is impossible without growth. A stagnant economy, therefore, means a stagnant public welfare system.

The important point about the socialist explanations for the gaps and failings of the welfare state is that they are limited and technical. The argument that there was a lack of tools to measure the effect of social policies or that there was a lack of clear objectives and adequate co-ordination or that the problem was a slow rate of economic growth, shows little or no sense of the potentially fundamental conflicts between the ethic of welfare and the values of capitalism.

Socialism and the welfare state

Is the welfare state the fulfilment of the socialist dream, the civilisation of capitalism and its reconciliation with socialism, or is it a truce based on conditions which will inevitably lead to further changes?

Tawney was quite clear that the development of a network of social services did not constitute socialism and would not on its own bring equality. Crucial to the attainment of both of these was the transfer of the key position of economic power to public control. Tawney stresses too that the socialist forgets his mission when he confines his efforts simply to altering the distribution of money and economic power. His aim is a social order of a different kind in which money and economic power will no longer be the criteria of achievement.[129]

Crosland concludes that the welfare state 'is not socialism'. It does fulfil some of the traditional socialist aspirations but 'it could clearly be a great deal more socialist than it is . . . since we could still have more social equality, a more classless society, and less avoidable social distress, we cannot be described as a socialist country.' The socialist will want to go beyond the welfare state because social distress and physical squalor still narrowly restrict the freedom of many individuals, because society is still disturbed by a great deal of social antagonism and class resentment and because the distribution of rewards and privileges, and the opportunity of attaining them remains highly inequitable.[130] In spite of these brave words, Crosland's concern is not really for a new kind of social order. When he sets out what the Labour Party really stands for in the 1970s he lists four key concerns – an exceptionally high priority for the relief of poverty, distress and social squalor; a more equal distribution of wealth; a wider ideal of social equality involving educational reform and a general improvement in our social capital; and finally strict social control of the environment to enable us to cope with the exploding problems of urban life.[131]

Elsewhere, certainly, Crosland declares a more radical philosophy.[132] But when the generalities are reduced to policy prescriptions they look much less radical. Of Crosland's four priorities for Labour, only the second — a more equal distribution of wealth — involves more than a modest extension and implementation of traditional welfare state goals.

Titmuss's vision of the good society certainly seems to go beyond the welfare state. His criticism of private welfare systems as a force both for perpetuating and exacerbating inequality and for concentrating unaccountable economic power implies a strong dislike of developments which have become an integral part of today's welfare state. The social philosophy outlined in 'The Gift Relationship' is, in its stress on fellowship, altruism, co-operation and service, a fundamental critique of capitalist society and involves criticisms which would be satisfied only by a new social order rather than an extended and refurbished welfare state.

A fundamental problem in trying to assess whether socialists see the welfare state as achieved socialism is the vagueness of the descriptions of what a socialist society would look like. The descriptions are no more than sketches. Concentration on immediate and obvious problems has inevitably aligned socialists with the development of the welfare state. Immediate needs and problems have led many to look no farther for the political battleground. Most have been preoccupied with immediate issues with only a glance beyond the struggles of the present.

Socialists are agreed in seeing the welfare state as an important influence for social change. While seeing their limited possibilities, Tawney nevertheless dismissed talk of the social services as 'mere palliatives' as 'a piece of claptrap'. He went on to explain their importance. 'A successful assault on the strongholds of capitalism', he wrote, 'demands a prolonged effort of intelligence and resolution. The more general establishment of the conditions of physical and mental vigour which even today can, if with difficulty, be carried forward, is not a minor issue. In so far as it is achieved, it dissolves the servile complex which is a capital obstacle to effective action. It is a step towards the creation of a population with the nerve and self-confidence to face without shrinking the immense task of socialist reconstruction.'[133] It is in this change of attitudes and aspirations that the social services make their long term contribution to the attainment of greater equality. 'By changing the lives of individuals and opening new possibilities to them, they change social psychology. The altered psychology acts as a permanent force modifying social structure, which, in turn, as it is transformed, sets minds and wills at work to insist on further modifications.'[134]

Crosland too sees the welfare state as providing a permanent dynamic influence for change because continually rising standards ensure that it always fails to satisfy the expectations which it generates. 'It thus breeds a permanent state of dissatisfaction which provides ammunition for those who want to argue that the whole approach has failed',[135] and, of course, for those who want more developments on similar lines.

T.H. Marshall argues in a very similar way though his argument is more generalised. Capitalism depends on inequalities to provide the dynamic to make it function but 'the preservation of economic inequalities has been made more difficult by the enrichment of the status of citizenship. There is less room for them, and there is more and more likelihood of their being challenged.'[136] The welfare state plays a key role in this, educating the public and the politicians about the continued existence of avoidable individual and social ills, all the time creating and inculcating new standards of welfare. It also trains and pays those whose professional task it is to criticise the ordering of economic and social life.

So while socialists see the welfare state as only the limited and partial achievement of some socialist goals, they are, nevertheless, optimistic about its influence. They see it not as dampening down the political forces making for further social change, but rather as a powerful ally raising aspirations, widening reference groups, illustrating and exacerbating the value conflicts of welfare capitalism and providing a dynamic for further change. In brief, they see the welfare state as an unstable compromise and a stepping stone toward socialism.

5

THE MARXISTS

It is not too inappropriate to begin a chapter on the Marxists' view of
the welfare state with a quotation from one of their arch enemies —
Hayek — for Marxists and liberals have both suffered at the hands of the
general public for their adherence to general principles. A quarter of a
century ago Hayek rejected gradualism and compromise in political
affairs in spite of the wide public support that these policies commanded.
'To advocate any clear-cut principles of social order is today an almost
certain way to incur the stigma of being an unpractical doctrinaire. It
has come to be regarded as the sign of the judicious mind that in social
matters one does not adhere to fixed principles but decides each
question "on its merits"; that one is generally guided by expediency and
is ready to compromise between opposed views.'[1] Hayek rejected
expediency and compromise because he felt that such policies were
leading Britain to socialism. The Marxists reject such policies for exactly
the opposite reason — they have delayed and perhaps made impossible
the creation of a socialist state in this country. Anti-collectivists and
Marxists disagree fundamentally on many issues but they are united in
their support of firm government policies based on undiluted political
principles. They view pragmatism as an ideology rather than as a value-
free political concept. They agree with Carr's dictum that 'to denounce
ideologies in general is to set up an ideology of one's own'.[2]

The Marxist view of the welfare state presented in this chapter stems
predominantly from the writings of Laski, Strachey and Miliband. The
writings of the first two span a period of over a quarter of a century —
from the mid-1920s to the mid-1950s — while Miliband's work is very
contemporary. No three writers can possibly represent fully all the

shades of Marxist opinion especially since they have not been consistent in their views. We are not, however, concerned here with a full and detailed exposition of Marxism but rather to note those of its aspects that are indispensable to the general understanding of the welfare state.

Social values

In spite of their materialistic explanation of historical events and social change, Marxists attribute a great deal of importance to society's value systems, as we shall see in the next section. What concerns us in this section, however, is their understanding of the three central values of socialism — liberty, equality and fraternity. To the Marxists, liberty is a broader concept than it is to the anti-collectivists. 'Liberty', wrote Laski, 'is a positive thing. It does not merely mean absence of restraint.'[3] Restraint is necessary and it is not a denial of liberty unless 'it frustrates the life of spiritual enrichment'.[4] He sees three aspects of liberty: private, political and economic. Seen as a composite concept, liberty cannot be achieved for the general public unless certain conditions prevail in society. First, liberty can never exist 'in the presence of special privilege';[5] second, 'where the rights of some depend upon the pleasure of others';[6] and third, where the incidence of State action is biased as it manifestly is under capitalism. Laski is, briefly, arguing that there cannot be liberty in a capitalist society for the mass of the people. In another context, he argues that the 'absence of equality and security from the context of freedom as the masses experience it means that the judgment of its reality is made on quite different premises by an unskilled labourer and a successful man of letters. They dwell in realms the contact between which is too fragmentary in character for a common interpretation of freedom to be normally valid for both.'[7] Freedom, in other words, without a substantial degree of economic security and equality is a hollow slogan. Freedom is tolerated but never fulfilled in a capitalist society. 'Liberty for us has been always hindered and hampered by its necessary subordination to the claims of property. It has been enjoyed only as its exercise has not threatened the owners of economic power.'[8]

Strachey, too, feels that civil liberties alone 'are for the workers, poor, thin and half-illusory things.'[9] They have to be complemented with economic liberty — freedom from fear of want, unemployment, and so on — and the presence of opportunity — 'opportunity to work, to earn, and so to live, and also to improve and develop themselves by study and to enjoy themselves.'[10] It is not that the traditional liberal type of freedom is rejected by Marxists but rather that it is found wanting and incomplete. Liberty and equality must therefore be seen as two necessary parts of a whole. The absence of equality in either the political or the economic field produces inequality in the other. 'Political equality . . . is never real', wrote Laski, 'unless it is accompanied by virtual economic equality; political power, otherwise, is bound to be the handmaid of economic power.'[11] Thus while for the anti-collectivists, liberty is almost synonymous with inequality, for the Marxists liberty is non-existent without equality of economic circumstances.

But what is equality? In broad terms, equality has been used to cover first 'the absence of special privilege'[12] and second that 'adequate opportunities are laid open to all'.[13] Thus equality does not mean sameness. It does mean, however, that 'such differences as exist must not be differences inexplicable in terms of reason. Distinctions of wealth or status must be distinctions to which all men can attain and they must be required by the common welfare.'[14] In a more specific sense, equality has been confined to economic power and economic rewards. It is this specific economic concept of equality that has attracted most discussion. Both Laski and Strachey are agreed that economic equality does not mean complete equality of incomes. Laski rejects this notion of complete income equality for three reasons: first, 'there seems no justice in an equal reward for unequal effort'; second, it does not 'seem just to reward equally where needs are unequal' and third, such a concept ignores 'the mental habits of western civilisation'.[15]

Laski also rejects, though with some reluctance, Marx's view that 'each contribute to society according to his powers and be rewarded by society according to his needs'.[16] He approves of the principle because it is based on moral foundations but rejects it because it is too simplistic and unworkable. Individual needs, he argues, are difficult to define. One has to adopt the notion of average needs for reasons of government policy. Even then, he is sceptical whether the government can justifiably be expected to meet all a person's needs at the average level. 'A clerk', he wrote, 'who decided to have thirteen children would have greater needs than a clerk with a family of four; but response to those needs is an undiscriminating endowment of stupidity.'[17] It is not only the concept of individual need but that of individual power or ability at work that is difficult to define. How are we to measure a person's power to perform a job? Since there is no objective measurement of a person's powers, we have no option but to rely on what the individual himself feels he can honestly do. Laski does not feel that this is an acceptable criterion. Hence, since we cannot define and measure individual power and need, the Marxist notion of equality must be rejected, claims Laski.

Laski's notion of economic equality is a relative form of equality. It attempts to satisfy 'the two complex conditions that it enables the individual to reach out towards his best self, while, simultaneously, it preserves and develops the necessary functions of society.' It attempts 'to reconcile the interest of the individual with that of the community'.[18] In practical terms this formula means first that 'every need related to the civic minimum, every need, that is, which when unsatisfied, prevents the attainment of effective citizenship, must be satisfied before we deal with needs above that civic minimum.'[19] Second, above the basic amount, differences in reward 'would be built either upon effort or ability',[20] to take account of the varying conditions in different occupations.

Strachey proposes two methods of rewards, one in the immediate aftermath of the collapse of capitalism and the other in the distant future when a communist society is achieved. From the short-term point of view, rewards ought to be 'in accordance with the quantity and the quality of the work done'.[21] In the long term, he supports the same Marxist view which Laski rejects, i.e. 'from each according to his ability and to each according to his need'. He explains, however, that before this form of reward can become a reality, society must have the technical know-how to create affluence of goods, and people must have gradually abandoned their capitalist acquisitive values for the egalitarian values of communism. The change of values, he feels, is a much more difficult proposition than the technological advancement of society.

Miliband is not explicit on his understanding of equality. His general discussion on poverty, however, indicates that, like the other two of our authors, he favours a reduction of income inequality and the nationalisation of large industrial and commercial enterprises. This is also the policy of the Communist Party of Great Britain as indicated in its various general election manifestos. In its manifesto for 1970, for example, it asked for the introduction of a minimum wage and wealth tax to reduce inequalities of income and wealth.[22]

In a recent interesting discussion on liberal and socialist values, Arblaster maintains that what divides liberals, conservatives and socialists is not so much that they hold different social values but rather their understanding of the same values and the priority that is given to different values by these groups. Thus, he maintains that apart from their differing understanding of social values, liberals treat freedom as the most central of their values, socialists ought to attribute this status to fraternity — one of the triumvirate of values of the French Revolution. Fraternity 'recognizes men's need for each other; and suggests that a good society will be one in which there are no longer any barriers to prevent men and women from living harmoniously and co-operatively with each other.'[23] It is in many ways a value that is antithetical to individualism. It views man as a social being, as co-operative, as a full member of his society in the sense that his thoughts and actions are influenced by those of his fellow-men and vice versa. This is a different conception of man and of society from that held by Hayek that was discussed in chapter 2. Government intervention is legitimate, necessary and beneficial from the conception of the social man. It is illegitimate, unnecessary and harmful from the conception of the self-contained individual. While other Marxists may not agree with Arblaster's elevation of fraternity to the apex of the value system hierarchy, it is clear that the Marxist interpretation of freedom and equality is better understood in the context of fraternity.

Societal organisation

'Socialist thinking must begin with the study of capitalism', wrote Strachey. This is the 'scientific' way of thinking as distinct from the dreamy, utopian thinking about societal organisation and change indulged in by various social reformers.[24] Strachey prefers to examine society by looking first at the economic structure, not because it is more important than the political or social structure but because it is 'the most get-at-able, the least illusive'.[25] Other Marxists would, however, insist with Marx that the economic structure is more important than the political and social structure. The way society earns its living accounts for the prevailing political system, the educational system, the position of women in society, art and so on. It also follows that changes in the modes of production, exchange and distribution of goods are the ultimate causes of all other change. This is not to say that the economic factor is the sole explanation of change but rather that it is the most important. 'Changes in the methods of economic production', wrote Laski, 'appear to be the most vital factor in the making of change in all the other social patterns we know.'[26] Other factors are also important but the part they will play, continues Laski, 'depends upon an environment, the nature of which is determined by its system of economic relationship'.[27]

It follows from this materialistic, economic explanation of society and of change that the position of the various groups in society vis-à-vis the economic system is paramount in explaining both the relationship between these groups and their attitude towards change. In any society, where the means of production are owned and controlled by one population group, conflict is inherent and inevitable. The struggle between the two main classes in capitalist society is not, Marxists insist, the figment of the imagination of revolutionaries but rather the natural outcome of a conflict situation. At an earlier period of his life, Strachey made this point quite clear: 'Communists and socialists', he wrote, 'do not cause, advocate, or like the class struggle: on the contrary, they diagnose the class struggle: they diagnose the class struggle as the essential and incurable sickness of modern society. The existing economic system compels the two main classes of modern society into conflict with one another. This is the reason why men are starving, clubbing, cheating and sometimes torturing each other. This is the reason, whether the participants in the struggle know it or not.'[28] The capitalist class wants to maintain the existing system intact since it works to its benefit while the radical section of the working class is anxious to change it since the whole working class suffers from its operation. This conflict between the classes is the fundamental cause of societal change for it reflects the conflict in the system of economic relations. There are, obviously, other forms of conflict in any society, apart from the conflict between capital and labour. There may be, for example, religious, ethnic or pressure group conflicts in any society but such conflict is of a different nature from class conflict because it is not centred around the means of production. The resolution of such conflict does not necessarily imply a change in the relation of the two classes to the means of production and hence to the economic, political and social system. To quote Laski, 'The distinction, which is ultimate, between all other social antagonisms and that between capital and labour is that the resolution of the latter can be achieved only by an alteration of the legal postulates of capitalist society.'[29]

In spite of this inherent conflict between the two main classes in society, the capitalist system has survived. Why? Three interrelated forces are said to have prevented the working class from using its vast numerical superiority over the ruling class to alter the economic and social system to its advantage: the economic power of the ruling class, the domination of the State apparatus by the ruling class and the legitimisation of a national ideology that fundamentally reflects the interests of the ruling class.

The wealth of the country and hence the levers of economic power are in the hands of a small minority of the population who control the small number of large enterprises that dominate the industrial and commercial life of the nation. Advanced capitalism, observed Miliband, 'is all but synonymous with giant enterprise and nothing about the economic organisation of these countries is more basically important than the increasing domination of key sectors of their industrial, financial and commercial life by a relatively small number of giant firms often interlinked.'[30] The managerial revolution has not had any fundamental effects on this process of the concentration of economic power in the hands of a small elite. Managers of modern corporations may conduct their business with additional aims in mind apart from profit but there is no denying, claim Baran and Sweezy, that 'profits, even though not the ultimate goal, are the necessary means to all ultimate goals. As such, they become the immediate, unique, unifying, quantitative aim of corporate policies, the touchstone of corporate rationality, the measure of corporate success.'[31] The 'soulful' corporation has not replaced the 'soulless' corporation as the exponents of the managerial revolution claim. Nor has the power of the managers overridden the power of the owners of wealth. There may be differences of opinion between these two overlapping groups but 'the fact remains that in any sense that seriously matters, it is not true that the managerial function alienates those who perform it from those on whose behalf it is performed; the differences of purpose and motivation which may exist between them are overshadowed by a basic community of interests.'[32]

This dominant class does not, of course, govern the country as it used to do in the old commercial city states of Venice or Genoa but it dominates major government decisions partly because of its economic power and partly because of the identity of its social origin, education and class situation with that of the political elite in the government, the civil service, the judiciary, the military and other arms of the State apparatus. The result is that the capitalist class does not govern but it rules.[33]

> In an epoch, when so much is made of democracy, equality, social mobility, classlessness and the rest, it has remained a basic fact of life in advanced capitalist countries that the vast majority of men and women in these countries has been governed, represented, administered, judged and commanded in war by people drawn from other, economically and socially superior and relatively distant classes.

The State apparatus is thus not a neutral umpire, arbitrating impartially between competing groups. 'It does not stand over and above the conflicting groups, judging impartially between them. By its very nature', wrote Laski, 'it is simply coercive power used to protect the system of rights and duties of one process of economic relationship from invasion by another class which seeks to change them in the interests of another process.'[34] The State will, of course, claim neutrality and impartiality. But this is a false claim in a society where one class owns most of the nation's wealth as well as the means of production. Social legislation is a peripheral activity of the State; its essential purpose is to protect the system of class-relations prevailing at any one time. In the case of capitalism, it is the protection of the interests of the capitalist class. It follows from this analysis that 'no state can secure the total well-being of a society unless the instruments of production are communally owned'.[35] Only in an egalitarian, undifferentiated society can the State be the servant of all citizens. In a capitalist society the State 'is simply a committee for managing the common affairs of the bourgeoisie' to use Marx's own words.

The concentration of economic power and the domination of the State by the small capitalist class could have been theoretically dismantled by the working class had it not been for the prevalence of a generally acceptable ideology that legitimises them. Such an hypothesis is, however, unscientific, the Marxists will argue, for ideology itself is a product of the existing system of class relations. It is natural for groups in society to produce value systems, which reflect their position in the class structure. There is nothing conspiratorial about this for people are usually the social products of their environment. A multiplicity of competing, or even worse, conflicting value systems, however, would make a society unstable, if not ungovernable. It is, therefore, necessary for one value system to become accepted as national and hence valued and obeyed by all sections of the community. What more natural than the fact that those 'who control an environment set the ideological quality of its life in a way, and to a degree, which involves hardly less those over whom they rule than it involves themselves. The rarest social type is the man who can transcend these familiar habituations.'[36]

Once a set of sectional values is legitimised into a national value system, it is sustained and propagated by the various institutions in society — the government, the church, the family, the school, the mass media, and so on. The value system is the product of the prevailing system of economic relations and hence, to quote Marx again, 'the ideas of the ruling class are in every epoch the ruling ideas.' The corollary of this is that the subordinate groups both aspire to the ruling ideology and, naturally, they learn to control themselves. This is a very depressing analysis, suggesting that the possibility of radical change is remote. Strachey had this in mind when he wrote that[37]

> the power of the capitalist class now rests predominantly upon their control over . . . the means of production of opinion, upon their control over men's minds. If this power to keep men in ignorance and unconsciousness of social processes could be removed, then the process of social transformation could be swift, easy and bloodless. The tragedy is that as long as their economic and political power remains, there exists no way by which the capitalists' hold over men's minds can be broken.

Even radical political parties and their leaders wittingly and unwittingly tailor their programmes to fit in to the dominant ideological framework. Miliband traces the development of the Labour Party, in and out of government, to demonstrate how it accommodated itself to the reigning ideology and how it has come to disclaim that it is the party of the working class. By arguing that it is pursuing policies that serve the 'national' interest and by playing down its class and socialist role, the

Labour Party has become not too dissimilar to the Conservative Party when in power.[38] Socialist ideology has given way to reformist ideology in the Labour Party and the trade unions. This is in line with Saville's argument that the dominant philosophy of the British working class has not been socialism but rather labourism, i.e. 'the theory and practice of class collaboration'.[39]

Value systems are never static, however. It would be untrue to argue that the values of the welfare state are exactly the same as the values of nineteenth-century England. Values inevitably change and such changes 'are caused by changes in social relationships, which, in their turn, are caused by changes in the material forces of production.'[40] Marxists, as mentioned earlier, do not insist that the economic factor is the sole avenue for change, though they do maintain that it is the most important. They do accept that there is 'a reciprocity of influence between the factors of social change'[41] so that values can be both a dependent and an independent variable. Indeed, radicals hold values which are not consonant with the prevailing system of economic relations though this system sets severe limits to the influence of such values in society. This circular relationship and, Marxists would claim, vicious circle between the economic system and the reigning ideology is a pretty deterministic model for change. Socialism, in other words, will replace capitalism when the economic circumstances are ripe. Laski accepted this without feeling that men have not a large part to play in this transformation. As he put it: 'While history presents men with their opportunities, it leaves them also to take advantage of them.'[42]

If men must seize their opportunities when these arise, the question of the appropriateness of means to achieve desirable ends becomes crucial. If men are not prepared to use any means when the conditions for change are ripe, then the opportunity for change may be lost for ever. It is in the context of this dilemma that the issue of the use of violence to achieve political ends can best be understood. There is nothing in the writings of the three authors to indicate any foolhardy encouragement of the use of violence to achieve their ends. On the contrary, they are apologetic about the use of violence and consider it only as a last resort. In the first place, they recognise that a violent action by the working class may turn out to be counter-productive as it is bound to bring forth a violent counter-action by the ruling class. Above all, however, they consider the peaceful road to socialism as superior to violence for, though it is bound to be a slow process, it will build a socialist society based on the consent of the majority of the people. This must imply such a change of public attitudes and values that will make the flourishing of a socialist society a spectacle for all mankind to admire. Reviewing the events of the 1930s and the second world war, Laski exemplifies this uncertainty regarding the role of violence for the achievement of socialism. 'It is possible, though I do not think it likely', he wrote, 'that if we organize for this end in time, we may persuade men . . . peacefully to acquiesce in this transformation. Certainly if we are successful in that persuasion, we shall have accomplished the most beneficent revolution in the history of the human race. It is on the other hand possible that the privileged will fight rather than give way.'[43] In spite of his slight inconsistencies on the use of violence, Laski always retained his faith in constitutional government and was loath to see it trampled on.[44]

> Where the members of a state enjoy fundamental political rights in a degree real enough to make effectively possible the transformation of dissent into orthodoxy, I believe that it is the duty of the citizen to exhaust the means placed at his disposal by the constitution of the State before resorting to revolution. I admit that the nature of capitalist democracy weights the scales unduly against him. I admit, also, that this is a counsel of prudent expediency rather than an ultimate moral right. But I believe that the gains which are inherent in the technique of constitutionalism are profounder, even though they are more slow, than those which are implicit in the revolutionary alternative.

Strachey, too, in his long list of publications adopted the same line as Laski towards the use of violence. Socialists 'abhor violence', he wrote, early in his life, 'but they may have to use it to defend themselves in the face of constant violence used by the ruling class.'[45] Later in his life, he held that the means used to achieve the ends affect the ends themselves. 'A socialism achieved by democratic means will inevitably be a basically different thing from a socialism achieved by dictatorial coercion.'[46] Indeed, it would be superior, for not only would it be based on the co-operation and participation of a consenting public, but also that it 'may prove a more complete solvent of every species of privilege than ever revolution has been'.[47]

It is true to say that over the years there has been a gradual loss of faith in the possibility as well as the advisability of using violence to achieve socialism in this country. The official policy of the Communist Party of Great Britain now is a peaceful parliamentary road to socialism. In one of its official documents the Communist Party states: 'There are now in some countries possibilities of winning political power without armed struggle. Such a peaceful, democratic advance to socialism can . . . be achieved in Britain.'[48] This position has not obviously gone unchallenged by contemporary Marxists. Warren, for example, feels that the official policy of the Communist Party confuses the issue.[49]

The crucial point is not the degree of physical violence but the necessity for a direct confrontation with the state power. Wise leadership and a popular movement which developed new forms of popular power able to confront capitalist state power and disarm it might with luck mean a peaceful transition. But this can never be equated with a parliamentary transition, the conception of which is a recipe for impotence and retreat.

Together with the increasing disapproval of violence to achieve political ends, there has grown, at best, an agnostic feeling and, at worst, a deep gloom on whether socialism will ever be achieved in this country. Laski succinctly posed the dilemma of a socialist government determined on drastic change forty years ago. If such a government[50]

goes slowly, it will suffer from all the difficulties which confront any government which tries, upon the basis of capitalist postulates, to effect their piecemeal transformation. It tends to irritate its opponents by undermining confidence and it fails to attract its supporters by inability to offer them the exhilarating spectacle of conviction turned into deed. If it proceeds rapidly . . . it is likely to meet with sabotage and resistance. In that event, it is dependent for its authority on the loyalty to its owners, not merely of the armed forces and the police but also of its own supporters whose security as wage earners is directly threatened by a dislocation of this kind.

In general, the prospects of any major changes taking place that would transform the welfare state into a socialist state are uncertain but they do not appear bright. Laski vaguely and perhaps wishfully remarked that 'the power of the rulers in our civilisation to deceive their subjects is, no doubt, profound but it is not a limitless power. I think that there is reason to suppose that its authority now approaches its final phase.'[51] Miliband, too, criticises Marcuse for his gloomy pessimism regarding the prospects of radical change in advanced industrial capitalist societies and vaguely hopes that sooner or later the working class will acquire 'the faculty of ruling the nation' which opens the road to socialism.[52] Finally, Strachey, too, felt that the struggle between the democratic institutions and the inherent tendencies of last stage capitalism towards greater inequality is unremitting and will be eventually resolved either by the suppression of democracy or the triumph of socialism. He hoped it would be the latter and remarked that 'service to the cause of democratic socialism requires, as does the service of every other great cause, an act of faith.'[53] If such service fails, it is better to have tried and failed than not to have tried at all. Generally, then, the welfare state may have created an impasse with no visible way round or through.

The role of government

It follows naturally from their emphasis on economic equality and the class conflict that Marxists would want the government to play a strong and active role in the social and particularly the economic aspects of society. Thus they are all agreed that economic 'equality' necessitates two other changes — industrial democracy and nationalisation of large industrial business and commercial enterprises. Nationalisaton of the means of production is justified on a variety of grounds. It is first considered immoral and anomalous that though profits are produced socially, i.e. through the work of the community and not through the work of individual shareholders, nevertheless, profits are distributed mostly to the few large shareholders. Moreover, these few individuals can decide whether to invest their profit or whether to spend it. It is true that taxation takes away from them some of their profit and influences their decision on what to do with the rest. Nevertheless, Strachey still considers this as 'one of those manifest scandals which, even if the economic loss involved is not so great as would at first sight appear, can hardly continue indefinitely once its existence is realised.'[54]

Second, the private ownership of the means of production clearly affects freedom as has been argued above. Laski argued that 'the private ownership of the means of production is no longer compatible with democratic institutions.'[55] This flows naturally from the class conflict analysis of society which all Marxists accept to a lesser or greater extent. Both Strachey and Laski agree that the abolition of functionless property and of the ever-growing concentration of power in fewer and larger firms is an absolute necessity for the survival of democracy. Strachey argued that though political power has been increasingly diffused, economic power has been increasingly concentrated during the last hundred years. Such trends, he felt, 'can hardly co-exist indefinitely. One must overcome and absorb the other; for political power and economic power are, in the last resort, merely aspects of one indivisible whole, namely power itself.'[56] Laski, too, felt that the emergence of 'a new caste of economic dictators' of large enterprises was a threat to democracy.[57]

> Their power is as massive in volume as it has largely been irresponsible in operation. We have reached a stage in historical evolution where either their power must be subordinated to the interest of the community or the interest of the community will be a tragic pseudonym to their power. Precisely as in the nineteenth century,

the irresponsible privilege of rentier and aristocrat was broken by the development of democracy in the political field, so in the twentieth century, we have to break the irresponsible privilege of rentier and plutocrat by the development of democracy in the economic field.

It is acknowledged that nationalisation measures cannot by themselves create a socialist society but it is argued that they are indispensable as a basis for further programmes. As Miliband concludes, nationalisation 'cannot by itself resolve all the problems associated with industrial society. What it can do, however, is to remove the greatest of all barriers to their solution and at least create the basis for the creation of a rational and humane social order.'[58]

All three writers are agreed that nationalisation of industry is necessary to achieve real industrial democracy which they all value very highly indeed. It is felt that industrial democracy extends and gives real meaning to political democracy; it reduces industrial conflict and promotes industrial co-operation between all sectors of an industry with the result that productivity benefits. Industrial democracy does not mean abolition of all authority in industry. What it means, according to Laski, is 'that the authority which exerts that power must be subject to the rules of democratic governance. It means the abrogation of unfettered and irresponsible will in the industrial world. It involves building decisions on principles which can be explained and the relation of those principles to the service any given industry is seeking to render.'[59] Laski's emphasis on the service which an industry should render to the community was part of his wider belief in the need to transform industries into professions. This would necessitate a reduction in the power of the owners of industry, if in private hands, the introduction of an industrial charter for the administration of industries on democratic principles, the introduction of qualification courses for all forms of work and general publicity about the affairs of all industries. In brief, industry 'needs to be informed by a principle of public service. It must not be merely a body of persons who are turning out goods for profit.'[60] This is a sentiment that was very dear to Tawney, too, as we saw in chapter 4. It also is today one of the main policy strands of the Communist Party of Great Britain. 'The big firms should be nationalised and run in the interests of the people, free from the burden of compensation and heavy interest payments. The governing boards should be made up of workers and technicians from the industry. Representatives of the employing class should be removed.'[61]

Government planning, with the widest and most varied form of participation, is, therefore, a central feature of a socialist society. Unlike the anti-collectivists who feel that there is far too much planning in the welfare state, the Marxists feel that there is not enough, particularly in the economic field. Planning is not seen as undermining individual freedom but rather as enhancing it. Laski, writing at the end of the last war, examined and rejected the three major arguments that planning leads to loss of freedom. The first argument is that 'economics . . . involves making decisions between the alternative uses of scarce means and that there must be a loss of freedom if, with the abandonment of the impersonal mechanism of the market, with objective price as the measure of supply and demand political authority intervenes to decide what shall one make and the price at which it is to be sold.'[62] Laski turns this argument on its head and points out that in a capitalist society, political authority is not neutral since it usually decides to allocate commodities according to the ability of people to pay rather than according to their urgent social need. In other words, the government decision not to intervene in the allocation of goods and the pricing of such goods is a political decision that benefits the better off in society. He feels that if 'political authority intervenes, as with rationing in war time, that is not necessarily a loss of freedom unless we define this to mean the right of the owners of property to use their economic power in any way they please.'[63]

The second argument against planning is this: 'Men . . . who are disposing of capital that is not their own lack the incentives to efficiency and inventiveness which, whatever its defects, the profit making motive supplies.'[64] Laski points out that this theory of the economic man is 'a compound of a particular theory of human nature and of the propaganda which an acquisitive society requires to protect itself from invasion by the principle of public ownership.'[65] He then goes on to argue that with a change in social values, with a change in the criteria which society adopts to apportion status to different jobs, and with adequate remuneration, any such difficulties which do exist can be overcome. Clearly, Laski implies that there is truth in the argument today and if the change from capitalism to socialism takes place quickly before social values change problems could arise.

The third argument is that in a planned society 'there is the risk that the governing group may take advantage of their position to acquire privileges for themselves which are not proportionate to the function they perform but to the power of which they dispose.'[66] Laski accepts that this is a danger in any society. But he dismisses it with scorn as being a danger to which only socialist governing groups are susceptible. This, he comments, 'is not a field in which the protagonists of capitalism can afford to take an attitude of superiority.'[67] If anything, socialist governments are less susceptible to such corruption than capitalist governments because of the egalitarian social values and the general ideology that prevails in socialist societies.

In general then, Marxists see central government planning as compatible both with efficiency and democracy. It is the form of planning that can best serve the interests of society. 'The characteristic of a planned democracy in a word', wrote Laski, echoing the others, 'will be the subordination of the market to a purpose or system of values upon which its members have agreed.'[68]

Both Laski and Strachey maintain that parliamentary democracy is compatible with and desirable in a socialist planned society. Political parties will operate within an ideological socialist framework. They are 'likely to differ from one another in the respective views they hold of the best way to develop the public estate from the angle of the values they accept.'[69] Political debate will not centre on issues of how to carve up the national cake between the social classes but how to promote different policies affecting the national interest. Theoretically, there is a place for a Conservative party too, but its ideas, states Laski, 'will operate in the society very much as the ideas of the Communist Party operate in a capitalist democracy. They will be tolerated so long as they are not regarded as a danger. They will be persecuted immediately they seem to threaten its foundations.'[70] The idea of the one-party socialist state has also been rejected by the Communist Party of Great Britain. Its general secretary has recently advocated the peaceful parliamentary way to socialism where a 'new type of parliament, with a majority of socialists and communists' would govern the country.[71] In such a socialist society, in addition to the Communist and Labour Parties, 'other political parties will have the right to maintain their organisatons, party publications and propaganda, and take part in elections to parliament and to local councils, provided that they conform to the law.'[72]

The welfare state

The welfare state, according to the Marxists, can only be understood properly if it is seen in the context of the class struggle. 'Social legislation', claims Laski, 'is not the outcome of a rational and objective willing of the common good by all members of the community alike; it is the price paid for those legal principles which secure the predominance of the owners of property. It waxes and wanes in terms of their prosperity. It is a body of concession offered to avert a decisive challenge to the principles by which their authority is maintained.'[73] Laski acknowledged that this was an undue simplification of a complicated process but still felt that it was a justifiable line of approach because it drew attention to the pivotal features of that process. It is important to emphasise that Marxists do not generally support the Machiavellian view of the welfare state, i.e. the view that the ruling class willingly and cunningly makes trivial concessions in advance in order to forestall heavy demands later from the working class. Rather they see social legislation as being forced out of the ruling class by working class pressure, either actual or potential. It is the ransom which the ruling class has had to pay for its survival. How much the ruling class will concede will depend on the dynamics of the particular situation in which the class conflict takes place.

The unity and strength of the working class is the first and obvious variable in this equation. It is no coincidence that most important social reforms have been won after the working class gained the right to vote. Conservative and Liberal governments, acting as the protectors of the interests of the ruling class, have been forced to introduce social reforms in order to gain the electoral support of the working class. Another important variable is the actual timing of working class pressures for reform. Laski warned the Labour Party repeatedly that unless it seized the opportunity at the aftermath of the last war when the working class and other sections of the population were united in their demand for change to introduce socialist legislation, it might have lost the opportunity for a peaceful road to socialism for ever. He warned that [74]

> if we have failed by the Armistice to lay the foundations of a revolution by consent, we shall pass rapidly to a position where because men no longer hold the great ends of life in common they will be unable to agree upon the methods of social change. In that event, the reorganisation of our basic principles will not be capable of accomplishment by peaceful means and the final disposition of forces will be determined not by discussion but by violence.

The state of the economy is another relevant consideration. The ruling class can afford to make concessions to working class demands at times of economic prosperity. It finds it increasingly difficult, however, during periods of economic stagnation or recession. In such difficult times, the working class will either topple the ruling class or, more likely, the ruling class will resort to force or to legalised forms of oppression in order to suppress the demands of the working class. In this way, both reform and repression are outcomes of the class struggle. The ruling class will use both measures to protect its interests depending on the state of play in the class struggle. Miliband thus concludes that reform and repression 'are not alternative options but complementary ones. However, as reform reveals itself incapable of subduing pressure and protest, so does the emphasis shift towards repression, coercion, police power, law and order, the struggle against subversion, etc.'[75]

The final and equally obvious factor in the struggle for reform is the nature of the demands made by the working class. Though the working class, because of its ideological subjugation to the upper class value system we discussed earlier in this chapter, does not usually make demands that threaten directly and immediately the status quo, it is bound to be resisted when it does so. No group in power has so far freely, knowingly and willingly legislated itself out of its privileges. The ruling class has been forced into conceding social reforms but it has kept its hold over the crucial area of the means of production so far. Whether it will ever surrender wealth and economic power peacefully is doubtful. If it does, according to the logistics of the class struggle, it will only be because the alternative would be far graver — its very physical demise. It is more than likely, however, that faced with demands that threaten its hegemony, the ruling class 'will, if it can, use the state power to suppress democratic institutions. I have, therefore, urged that, at this stage of economic development, the difference between classes can only be settled by force.'[76]

Marxists are agreed that in spite of its origins, the social reform movement has delayed and perhaps averted for good the collapse of capitalism. It has done this by removing some of the glaring excesses of capitalism, i.e. by humanising it, and thus making it more acceptable to ordinary working people. This is held to be true in spite of the fact that most social reforms had been opposed by entrenched interests. Reviewing the post-war social policy legislation of the Labour government, Miliband observes that these measures 'represented of course a major, it could even be said a dramatic, extension of the system of welfare which was part of the "ransom" the working classes had been able to extract from their rulers in the course of a hundred years. But it did not, for all its importance, constitute any threat to the existing system of power or privilege. What it did constitute was a certain humanisation of the existing social order.'[77] Thus, social policy legislation, by reducing tensions, promotes social cohesion and thus makes continuity and stability of the social system possible.

It is not only because of the de-radicalisation effect that social reform has on the working class that it has safeguarded the capitalist system. We referred earlier to the modest claims of social reforms. What Marxists claim is that even modest reforms are not implemented to the full, they are thwarted in their implementation with the result that they deliver less than they promise. The net result of these involved operations is that the same social problems lumber on in capitalist societies in spite of continuous government efforts to eradicate them. Miliband thus concludes that 'reform always and necessarily falls far short of the promise it was proclaimed to hold: the crusades which were to reach "new frontiers" to create "the great society", to eliminate poverty, to abolish the class struggle, to assure justice for all, etc., etc., – the crusades regularly grind to a halt and the State comes under renewed and increased pressure.'[78]

Finally, reforms in the economic field, such as government aid to industry, family income supplements to low-paid workers, etc., have become parts of a complicated process of generally managing the economy. This is the economic role of public spending. Barratt Brown concludes that public spending 'appears now to consist not only of managing the economy to maintain aggregate demand for full employment, not only by more state spending and by some very modest redistribution of income, but also by protecting a bottom layer in society whose position is continuously being worsened and tends to pull down the whole level of aggregate demand.'[79]

Marxists are not against reforms per se though they would prefer bolder, more radical measures. They cannot but accept the fact that despite their timidity, social reforms have contributed to the improvement in the standard of living of the working class. Even in such areas as economic inequality, where the evidence tends to show that little progress has been made, Strachey argues that the situation would have been worse had it not been for the effects of State intervention. He bases his argument on the thesis 'that capitalism has, in fact, an innate tendency to extreme and ever growing inequality. For how otherwise could all these cumulative equalitarian measures which the popular forces have succeeded in enacting over the past hundred years have done little more than hold the position constant?'[80]

Moreover, social reform is the only type of socialism that people understand and are prepared to support. Abstract socialism is only a dream aspired to by a few. It has to be itemised into individual concrete reforms to attract the support not only of working class but of liberal sympathisers as well. Referring to the frustrations and disappointment of some of the Labour Party supporters in the 1930s, Strachey warned that only pragmatic socialist programmes were politically viable. To abandon such programmes for an all-or-nothing campaign in order to achieve complete socialism would be a political suicide.[81]

A frequent reaction to a realisation of the inevitability of capitalist resistance on the part of the left of the Labour movement has been to conclude that it is useless to put forward any programme of social reforms; that the movement ought to demand Socialism or nothing. But this is a wholly unjustified position. What experience has shown is that, in contemporary conditions, it is impossible to carry through a programme of social reforms, without a severe struggle with the dominant capitalist interests. But this fact must certainly not be allowed to prevent the movement putting forward its programme of social reform and carrying it through in the face of that opposition.

To confine the movement's propaganda to the bare demand for Socialism, without voicing and being absolutely determined to satisfy men's simple demands for a decent standard of life, for democracy and for peace, would be to reduce ourselves and our movement to sterility.

Finally, the Marxists' approval of social reforms stems from the belief that the welfare state has helped to raise people's expectations in life and that every step forward is a base from which further improvements and further demands for change can be made. It is exactly the same process which the anti-collectivists have condemned that the Marxists approve. Laski insists that rights are relative to the period in which they are being implemented and that there is, therefore, no final, definite fulfilment of such rights.[82]

When we say, therefore, that the State must secure to each citizen the conditions under which he can fulfil himself as a moral being, we must realise that those conditions are not permanent, but relative to an environment perpetually changing; and the level at which the conditions must be secured is invariably a function of that environment. We can never arrest, as it were, some given moment of time and make its possibilities a criterion of reasonable expectation. Dynamic experience plays havoc with our standards of fulfilment.

Strachey was understandably more emphatic on the positive effects of the welfare state on public feelings of relative deprivation in the mid-1950s. He argued that the establishment of the welfare state in the post-war years conferred 'rights' on ordinary people and it, therefore, enlisted their support for its protection and expansion. 'Once such "rights" as these have been acquired', he maintained, 'democracy becomes much more strongly entrenched than before. For then the struggle to maintain and extend democracy can be undertaken as a struggle to preserve known, tangible and valued rights and not merely as a struggle to achieve theoretically desirable ideals.'[83] The welfare state has both conforming and vitalising effects on the attitudes of the general public. It makes people both more accepting of capitalism but also more likely to defend their standard of living and to demand improvements. By implication, when capitalism reaches the point where it cannot fulfil people's rising aspirations, it will reach its final crisis point which may either necessitate repressive measures or lead to its downfall.

None of our three writers looks at individual social services. Unlike the anti-collectivists who have examined individual social services in detail and have put forward alternative solutions, Marxists have stood aloof on this issue. From what little has been written by Marxists and from the election manifestos of the Communist Party of Great Britain, however, it can be safely said that the Marxist view of individual social services is very similar to the Fabian view. In education, the main demands are comprehensive schools, nursery education, expansion of higher education, reduction in the size of classes, more and better-paid teachers and the abolition of public schools.[84] In housing, there have been suggestions for the nationalisation of urban land for house building purposes, low interest rates to local authorities and owner-occupiers, restriction of private landlordism and greater legal security for all tenants against eviction and harassment. Fundamentally, however, it is accepted that owner-occupation is acceptable in a socialist society. The National Health Service is generally treated as a better specimen of socialist welfare provision than the other social services. Apart from improvements in buildings and manpower and the abolition of all charges and of private practice within the National Health Service, there is little fundamental criticism of the Service apart from Rossdale's work. He explores the inter-relationship between illness on one hand and the physical, social and work environment on the other and argues that to deal effectively with illness one must do likewise with man's total environment. This must involve a wider role for doctors as well as a demystification of that role, a more egalitarian doctor-patient relationship.[85]

Because of its association with income distribution and with poverty, the social security service has perhaps received more attention and more criticism than the other social services. Kincaid has written fairly extensively on this though his proposals may not of course be acceptable to other Marxists. His fundamental principle for social security benefits is universality. This means the abolition of the insurance principle and means tests. The first excludes many people from receiving benefits as of right while selectivity 'is a recipe for the creation of second-class citizens.'[86] Benefits, of adequate standard, must be paid to all who fall into certain need-producing situations, i.e. unemployment, sickness, old age, etc.

Though Marxists may not differ substantially from Fabians on their critique of individual social services, they differ in the faith they place in the ability of the welfare state to solve the problems of poverty, bad housing, inequality in education and so on. Marxists, unlike Fabians, maintain that the welfare state, by its very nature, cannot abolish poverty and inequality either in income or in housing or in political power because to do so would imply a defeat of the ruling class. It may modify but it cannot solve the main social problems for these are rooted in the class structure of society. Miliband maintains, for example, that[87]

talk of the 'elimination of poverty' is no more than an illusion or a deception. Something can be done by an even modestly reforming government. But the truth — and it is a bitter truth — is that the abolition of poverty will have to wait until the abolition of the system which breeds it comes on to the agenda and this is a question which far transcends the issue of poverty itself.

Barratt Brown takes a similar line not only in relation to poverty but to other social problems. He concludes his discussion on the welfare state by saying that[88]

limited though they may be in achieving 'an ideal output', welfare state measures do confer real benefits which each individual's pursuit of his own satisfaction through the market would not have achieved. The state in assuring these benefits enforces a conformity or consensus upon all citizens about those public benefits that are to be conferred and those that are not, and about the cost that is to be paid for them. Consensus politics is then concerned with fairly minor variations in the benefits to be provided. It is not concerned with great inequalities of wealth.

In brief, the welfare state cannot solve the social problems of today without the abolition of the capitalist system. We devote most of the next chapter to the discussion of this fundamental question.

6

Social justice and social policy

So far we have confined ourselves mainly to analysing the attitudes of various groups of thinkers to the role of the State in welfare. In this last chapter we set out our own interpretations of the welfare state and of its successes and failures.

The failure of the welfare state since the war

One of the most striking aspects of the development of social policy since the second world war has been the failure to achieve aims which were accepted as fundamental in the years between 1944 and 1948. The failure is not failure in terms of the extravagant hopes of optimistic radical reformers or starry-eyed academics. It is failure in terms of the explicit aims enshrined in statute or in the speeches of those responsible for inaugurating or restructuring the services.

We are not arguing that no progress has been made. Such an argument would clearly be absurd. Important advances have been made in all services but these advances have, in all cases, fallen well short of the not unreasonable objectives set in the past. A brief look at the major services illustrates this point.

The purpose of the National Health Service, Jennie Lee told the 20th Anniversary Conference, was 'to ensure that everybody in the country irrespective of means, age, sex or occupation, should have equal opportunity to benefit from the best and most up to date medical and allied services available'.[1] This objective, which could hardly be described as extravagant, has not been achieved. The geographical distribution of medical services is still extremely unequal. A glance at the distribution of hospital services shows that although the inequalities which existed in the early years of the service have been reduced in some respects, the discrepancies which remain are striking. In 1950-1, the range of expenditure in regional hospital boards was from 143 per cent of the national average to 71 per cent. In 1971-2, the range was from 112 per cent to 84 per cent. For both years, the South West Metropolitan and the Sheffield Regional Hospital Boards were the highest and the lowest spending areas respectively.[2] Most of the narrowing which has been achieved has come in fact in recent years. The introduction in 1971 of a new formula for allocating resources should lead to a further narrowing of the gap.

The regional inequalities obviously extend from finance to the provision of the various hospital resources. The overall number of hospital beds per 1,000 population varies considerably and the gap has scarcely closed in the last twenty-five years. The same applies to psychiatric beds and there is an even greater range in the case of geriatric and chronic beds. Another 'proxy of quality' for the hospital service is the distribution of consultant merit awards. It is a fallible index in various ways but, given its limitations, it suggests that if you are going to need specialist treatment it is very advantageous to live in certain areas and very disadvantageous to live in others.[3]

There are great variations in staffing between Hospital Boards. The number of senior medical and dental staff per 1,000 hospital beds varies from 33.3 in the Oxford region to 21.3 in Leeds. They are supported by an equally uneven provision of nursing and midwifery staff – 632 per 1,000 beds in Oxford compared with 556 in Leeds.[4] Maynard's detailed examination of the staff available per 100 residents in mental illness and mental handicap hospitals in the different Regional Hospital Boards emphasises this point. He found that there were more than twice as many consultants in psychiatry and three times as many psychologists in Oxford as in the South West. Oxford had one and a half times as many nursing staff as East Anglia and three times as many social workers.[5] In mental handicap hospitals it was the same startling picture of contrasts between the best and the worst.

Another aspect of the geographical pattern of medical services is the distribution of general practitioners. This was a matter of concern during the discussions which preceded the creation of the National Health Service and in the years since 1948 the government has used two kinds of approach to the problem: that of negative direction making it difficult or impossible for new doctors to establish themselves in certain areas already well doctored, and second, that of offering positive incentives to doctors to move to under-doctored parts. In Butler's view, however, this policy has not been pursued with force or purpose or with effective co-ordination of its various elements.

Nevertheless, there has been a narrowing of the gap between the best off and the worst off areas, the result of a fall in list sizes in the designated areas and a rise in the restricted areas.[6] The basic pattern of distribution however, Butler concludes, has remained 'largely unaltered over the past thirty years . . . Areas which are currently facing the most serious shortages seem to have a fairly long history of manpower difficulties, while those which are today relatively well supplied with family doctors have generally had no difficulty in past years in attracting and keeping an adequate number of practitioners.'[7] Of special importance is Butler's evidence that the smaller the geographical unit used for assessing the fairness of the distribution of general practitioners, the greater the inequality of distribution. For the patient — or would-be-patient — the local situation is what matters — how easy it is for him to get on to a doctor's list and how easy it is for him to visit, or be visited by, his doctor.

With regard to General Practitioners something has been attempted and something has been achieved. The distribution of dentists has not, however, been a matter on which the government has sought to achieve greater equality of distribution. The result is that the geographical distribution of dentists is much more unequal than the distribution of General Practitioners and there has been little or no progress towards greater equality.[8] Cook and Walker describing the situation in the early 1960s found a clear association between the distribution of dentists and the social class structure of the area — the higher the proportion of the population in the top socio-economic group, the higher the proportion of dentists and conversely, the higher the proportion of semi-skilled and unskilled workers, the lower the proportion of dentists.[9]

Another aspect of the geographical distribution of medical services is the services provided by local authorities. The range of expenditure in 1971 was wider for local authorities than for Regional Hospital Boards. The four highest spending county boroughs averaged 130 per cent of the national average while the four lowest averaged 76 per cent. In the last twenty years the gap between highest and lowest spenders has altered only slightly. In 1952-3 the four highest spending county boroughs averaged 135 per cent of the national average and the four lowest averaged 67 per cent.[10] These facts endorse Morris's judgment that 'The freedom of Local Authorities should extend only to the provision of services above nationally accepted standards.'[11]

The injustice of the unequal distribution of health care resources is plain. As Coates and Rawstron recently pointed out,[12]

the National Health Service was designed to cater for all the people.

Twenty years after its inauguration the unequal geographical distribution of resources means that many people are (a) leading more limited lives than is necessary, (b) submerged in the 'clinical iceberg', and (c) dying because of the failure to allocate resources to counteract regional imbalance in housing, pollution, dereliction, education and health and welfare services. In reality, some regions are allowed to be 'more equal than others'.

Another criterion implicit in Jennie Lee's statement of the aims of the National Health Service is equality of consideration for all patient groups. In the twenty years after 1948 the ratio of expenditure per patient in the acute hospitals and in the long-stay chronic hospitals changed scarcely at all though there has been some improvement during the last five years. Thus the weekly cost of patients in mental deficiency and mental illness hospitals in 1951 was 21 per cent of the cost of patients in general hospitals; in 1973 it was 37 per cent. Clearly a start has been made but the more detailed evidence of the cost of different patient groups today suggests that the journey will be long and hard — particularly in a period of economic stringency. Thus the total weekly cost per in-patient in hospitals in 1972-3 was £91.54 for acute illness; £79.60 for mainly acute; £65.97 for partly acute; £49.97 for mainly long-stay; £40.25 for long-stay; £30.34 for mental illness; and £28.02 for mental handicap.[13]

From the evidence it is clear that the objective of equality of access to medical care has not been achieved. It is equally plain that in the first twenty years of the service little positive effort to equalise access was undertaken. The issue is not one simply of shortages of resources but of the distribution of resources and of a commitment to certain ends.

The fundamental aim underlying the 1944 Education Act was to secure equality of opportunity to children wherever they lived or whatever the income, class or race of their parents. The English educational system has manifestly failed to achieve this. As with other local authority services, there are differences between education authorities which are explicable only in terms of widely different standards of provision.

Over the years the Department of Education and Science has operated a quota scheme to try and ensure an even distribution of full-time teachers throughout the country. The latest figures, however, show a range in teacher costs per primary pupil in County Boroughs from 110 per cent of the national average in York to 87 per cent of the national average in Barrow-in-Furness. The implication must be that children in York are either getting more teachers, or better qualified teachers or more experienced teachers than their contemporaries in Barrow. In secondary schools the range is from 130 per cent of the national average in Southampton to 78 per cent in Bootle. Part of this difference is due to the differing proportions of pupils staying beyond school leaving age, as sixth formers are much more expensive to teach, but even allowing for this the range is striking.

In the latest statistics a block sum for 'Teaching Aids' is recorded rather than separate sums for books, educational equipment, etc. But in 1971-2, when expenditure on books was recorded separately, expenditure in primary schools ranged from 227 per cent of the national average to 48 per cent and in secondary schools from 184 per cent to 63 per cent. Here are solid, tangible differences in the provision of vital education tools. The broader heading of Teaching Aids shows the same sort of range — from 151 per cent of the national average per primary child in Carlisle to 51 per cent in Brighton and from 17 per cent of the national secondary average in Southampton to a beggarly 49 per cent in Brighton.

Progress towards greater equality of expenditure between County Boroughs has been slight in the last twenty years. In 1952-3 the total figures for expenditure per primary child ranged from 159 per cent of the national average to 81 per cent, from 125 per cent of the secondary average to 78 per cent.[14] In 1972-3 the range in expenditure per primary child was from 118 per cent of the national average in Stoke to 86 per cent in Southport, from 135 per cent of the secondary average — again in Stoke — to 84 per cent in Bootle.[15] These variations are a crude but significant index of variations in the extent and quality of local authority provision. When all possible explanations have been taken into account it is plain that different local education authorities are spending very different amounts of money and it may reasonably be assumed that the outcome is services of very varying qualities. Some children are clearly being disadvantaged.

The extent to which children are advantaged by better educational provision is a matter for argument. Jencks's conclusion is that no specific school resource has a consistent effect on test scores or eventual educational attainment. Byrne and Williamson, on the other hand, have sought to show 'that the provision of educational resources in an area may be a significant factor in explaining variations in school attainment of different social groups.'[16] Whether or not Byrne and Williamson are correct is, in a sense, unimportant for the argument about the need for equality of provision because Jencks accepts that, though increased expenditure 'cannot then be justified on the grounds that it makes life better in the hereafter . . . it can be justified on the grounds that it makes life better right now.'[17]

Inequalities in expenditure between local education authorities give a broad picture of inequalities of provision. The figures for total local authority spending tell nothing, of course, about how resources are allocated between schools. Parsimonious authorities may allocate their meagre resources with justice, high spenders with injustice.

Implicit in the Newsom and Plowden Reports, however, is the conclusion that inequalities between schools have been allowed to develop and continue − in particular, that in the post-war years inner city children have been treated unjustly in comparison with many of those who have moved to new estates and new towns. The first consideration for any local education authority must be roofs over heads and desks under elbows. Rehousing programmes therefore commit local education authorities to particular patterns of expenditure and to a greater concern for the needs of the mobile rather than the immobile. Until 1967 there was no thought that the immobile, inner city school should be compensated. Education policy aiming at equality of opportunity, however, would seek to provide a genuine parity of resources between schools, seeking to compensate the down at heel down-town school with more generous allocations of other kinds of resources.

The great bulk of research in the sociology of education in this country has been concerned with the varied performances of the children of different social groups. It has revealed wide ranging inequalities of opportunity. The National Child Development Study, for example, showed that the chances of an unskilled manual worker's child being a poor reader at age seven are six times greater than for a professional worker's child.[18] At the same age the difference in reading attainment between children from Social Class I and II and those from Class V was equivalent to seventeen months of reading age. Other research has shown how, of middle and working class children who were of equivalent measured ability at age eight, significantly more middle class children gained grammar school places three years later.[19] Once at grammar school working class children do less well than middle class children of equivalent ability at age eleven. They are more likely to end up in low streams, to leave early without any external examination passes.

In spite of the great expansion in sixth form education in the 1960s the social class composition of sixth forms changed little. They remained middle class institutions. In the universities, however, Glennerster shows a small decline in inequality of access. In 1960 boys from non-manual backgrounds had six times the chance of boys from manual backgrounds of going to university but by 1968 their chance was only four times as great. The position of working class girls improved too − from having one-thirteenth of the chance of going to university of their middle class contemporaries in 1960, their chance had improved to one-tenth by the end of the decade.[20]

To labour the point would be tedious. What is all too apparent is that equality of opportunity has not been achieved. Class and sex are still sources of major inequality and injustice. Regional differences in the

numbers of sixteen-year-olds still at school in 1972 — 41 per cent in
the south-east, 29 per cent in the north-west — reflect these continuing
inequalities.[21]

If we accept that equality of opportunity is unattainable in an unequal
society, nevertheless in an unequal society a just education system
would seek in all possible ways to mitigate inequalities and to give each
child an equal opportunity to acquire intelligence and to realise his
potential. To what extent has the English educational system vigorously
pursued such policies?

Such an approach means positive discrimination in both primary and
secondary schools so that extra resources are channelled to schools with
special needs 'going well beyond an attempt to equalise resources'.[22]
Plowden called for 2 per cent of the most deprived primary schools to
be given priority in the first year of a new priority programme, the
number to rise to 10 per cent within five years.[23] Seven years after the
publication of the Plowden Report less than 3 per cent of primary
schools have been designated as priority schools. In spite of concern
about comprehensive schools condemned to draw their pupils from
areas of environmental difficulty, no attempt has been made to extend
the idea to secondary schools — though Benn and Simon suggested it as
one answer to the problem.[24] As Glennerster argues, 'To take positive
discrimination seriously means adopting it as a total strategy, adopting
it at every level of education, in every area, in schools as well as
between schools, out of schools as much as in school.'[25]

The record of the English educational system in the area of policies
to secure equality of opportunity is a gloomy one. Halsey's conclusion
is that 'the essential fact of twentieth century educational history is
that egalitarian policies have failed.'[26] This is certainly true. Equally
true is the fact that there has been no concerted effort to devise and
adopt policies to combat known inequalities. Policies with equalising
intentions and implications have certainly been adopted — for example
comprehensive reorganisation and the EPA programme but there has
been no overall strategy, no attempt to isolate critical points of intervention, no attempt to deal with obvious straightforward issues such as
reform of the eccentricities of the educational maintenance allowance
system.[27]

In the field of social security the recommendation of the Beveridge
Report which captured the imagination of the nation was that the State
should guarantee a minimum standard of living for all its citizens. In
the years since the 1946 National Insurance Act many changes have
been made in the income maintenance service. In many ways it has
become more sensitive and responsive to the varied patterns of need of
one-parent families, the disabled, the elderly, the low paid and so on.
Nevertheless the vital comment on its operation is that poverty, as

officially defined, has not been abolished in British society. The proportion of the general population living below the official poverty line has remained fairly constant in the last twenty-five years. The level of social security benefits has been raised many times but only to take account of the rise in prices or wages. The amount of flat rate benefits constitutes the same proportion of average earnings today as it did in 1948. It is true that benefits are now raised automatically every year to catch up with inflation but not to improve their position vis-à-vis the earnings of people at work. As regards the low paid worker, the Family Incomes Supplement meets only part of the difference between the individual's wage and his assumed needs. A safe gap has to be left to act as an incentive. Not only, however, has poverty not been abolished. Its incidence has not changed significantly. The old and the low paid are still the two main groups in poverty. There is still a poverty cycle for many of the low paid as there was in Rowntree's time. The low paid worker of today is the impoverished retirement pensioner of tomorrow.

Similarly, efforts to reduce inequalities of income and wealth have borne little fruit. Thus the earnings of the lowest decile of full time adult male manual workers constituted 68 per cent of the median weekly earnings of male manual workers in 1886, 69 per cent in 1960 and after almost ten years of government activity to help the low paid, 65 per cent in 1973. Both trade unions and governments have paid lip service to the condition of the low paid but they have never made the improvement of their condition a top priority of their activities. Another index of the extent of income inequality is the difference in incomes between the highest and the lowest paid members of society. The top 1 per cent of income earners receive 8 per cent of income before tax; the top 10 per cent receive 29 per cent whereas the bottom 20 per cent get less than 7½ per cent, i.e. slightly less than the top 1 per cent. There has been no inherent general trend towards greater equality of income distribution. There have been short periods, usually during war time, when income inequalities have been slightly reduced only to be offset in subsequent years.

The distribution of wealth is even more unequal than the distribution of income. Although there are differences in the various estimates of the distribution of wealth, the broad picture is clear. In 1970, 1 per cent of the population owned 24-30 per cent of personal wealth and the top 5 per cent owned 45-56 per cent of the wealth.[28] There has been some apparent redistribution of wealth during this century although part of this redistribution has been mainly from the very rich to the rich.[29] It is also quite possible that to some extent this movement of wealth is an intra-family affair, the result of efforts to avoid the payment of death duties. The evidence that younger age groups and women now own more wealth than in the past lends support to this view.

To what extent, finally, has housing policy since the war fulfilled its aims? As a statement of the aims of policy we can perhaps take a sentence from the Conservative government's 1973 White Paper. 'The ultimate aim of housing policy', the White Paper declares, 'is that everyone should have a decent home with a reasonable choice of owning or renting the sort of home they want.'[30] Implicit in this declaration of intent are aims about supply and availability of housing, the quality of housing, choice of type and tenure and the distribution of subsidies.

There has clearly been a marked change in the tenure of housing — a substantial increase in privately owned as well as council housing at the expense of the private rented sector.[31] This trend, however, has not increased people's choice in housing. Market forces and not choice or need determine the type of housing of families in Britain. Thus social class is a root factor to the tenure of housing: the higher social classes are more likely than the working classes to be owner-occupiers; less likely to be in local authority or in privately rented unfurnished housing. It is only in the privately rented furnished housing that there is no such statistical relationship, though this is a statistical illusion for in practice the upper classes occupy the best and the working classes the worst of such housing. Though a higher proportion of working class people are owner-occupiers today than previously, they obviously own the less desirable type of private housing. 'Detached houses', says a recent government survey, 'were the type lived in by almost half the house-holds of professional workers, compared with only 4 per cent of unskilled workers' households, while terraced houses displayed the opposite pattern.'[32]

There has been a decline in overcrowding however one measures it. If one uses the number of persons per habitable room (including kitchens) as the yardstick of overcrowding, then the improvement in the situation is clear in spite of the fact that part of this improvement is due to a decline in the size of households. This standard of housing, moreover, takes no account of the size or the structural condition of the rooms. In spite of these qualifications, the number of persons per room was 0.86 in 1931, 0.76 in 1951, 0.68 in 1961 and 0.63 in 1971.[33] If one adopts a more generous standard of housing density, i.e. the bedroom standard, which allocates a standard number of bedrooms to each household according to certain rules, the picture is still the same though not as rosy. The proportion of overcrowding, according to this definition, dropped from 11 per cent in 1960 to 6 per cent in 1971 in England and Wales.

This improvement, though real and meaningful, has not eliminated social class differences in overcrowding. There is still a strong inverse relationship between social class and overcrowding. Using the bedroom standard, 1 per cent of the professional socio-economic groups were overcrowded, while the proportions for the skilled and the unskilled groups were 8.5 per cent and 11 per cent respectively in 1971.[34] The improvement in this aspect of housing masks obviously substantial regional differences, with London and Scotland at the top of the over-crwoding table both today and in 1950.

For over ten years now the number of dwellings and the number of housing units has been roughly in balance. This gives, however, a misleading picture. Nationally there may seem to be no overall shortage of housing but there are still extreme local shortages, particularly in the conurbations and most of all in London. In London in the last few years local authority waiting lists have been growing. Supply is way behind demand or need.

The most compelling index of shortage is the number of persons officially registered as homeless. Statistics are scanty and they grossly underestimate the degree of homelessness. They cover only those persons known to local authorities, with the result that such groups as the single homeless are virtually ignored in the statistics. They also refer to the number of persons registered as homeless on one night rather than the total number of homeless persons during the year. Also, they do not take into account the number of children received into care because of homelessness. Finally, they do not include any of the families who apply for admission to temporary accommodation and who are refused. For what they are worth, the official statistics show that the number of people in temporary accommodation for homeless persons increased from 11,000 in 1966 to 25,000 in 1972.[35] Half the number in 1972 and three-quarters in 1966 were in the area of Greater London. Social policy for homeless people has always been unsatisfactory. The responsibility of local authorities for homeless persons under the National Assistance Act, 1948, was not as clear-cut and mandatory as it ought to have been. The Local Government Act, 1972, seems to have weakened the position of the homeless vis-à-vis the local authorities even more. This is hardly the way to tackle a problem which on any criteria should not be tolerated in an affluent society.

On the issue of quality and possession of the basic housing amenities there has been a marked improvement in the last twenty-five years, so that over the whole country only 9 per cent of households had no bath and 3 per cent shared one in 1972. In the same year the corresponding figures for toilets were 1 per cent and 3 per cent respectively. The relationship between social class and lack of these basic housing amenities is again evident though not so striking because council housing compares very well with privately owned houses in this respect. It is the privately rented, unfurnished housing which suffers most from the lack of these amenities: 38.3 per cent of households in privately

115

rented unfurnished dwellings had no bath and 6.4 per cent shared one; 3.9 per cent had no WC and 8.8 per cent shared one in 1972. As was mentioned earlier, it is mainly working class families that live in unfurnished, privately rented accommodation. Other evidence shows further that it is the weaker sectors of the working class – the unskilled and the fatherless families – that occupy this type of housing. It is worth pointing out that there is also a clear association between overcrowding and lack of amenities, with the result that housing handicaps compound each other. As with other indices of housing stress and hardship the situation is worst in London. Ten thousand families between Finsbury Park and Archway still lack the three basic housing amenities – a bath, hot water and an inside WC.[36]

The sentiments expressed in the sentence quoted above from the Conservative White Paper depend for their translation into reality on a system of housing subsidies of some kind or other. Few people are in a position to pay the true contemporary cost of their housing. For twenty-five years after the war subsidies were of two kinds – tax relief on mortgage interest for the owner-occupier, and subsidised rents to council tenants made possible by Exchequer and rate subsidies. There was no help to the private tenant. The average owner occupier with a mortgage has consistently received more help with his housing costs than the average council tenant.

Commenting on the favourable treatment of owner occupiers, the NALGO Housing Working Party rightly concluded that it has[37]

two undesirable features: first, an important part of real income is effectively untaxed and the subsidy is regressive in that it gives most to those who already earn most. Second, it encourages housing demand by the rich as a form of investment and it drives building resources and land to the rich end of the market as against the poor end and by encouraging building for owner occupation, housing resources have been channelled away from areas of greatest need.

The position of the council tenant was further complicated by the Housing Finance Act, 1972. This Act made it compulsory for local authorities to provide rent rebate schemes for their tenants and it went so far as to lay down standards which all local authorities had to adopt in their rent rebate schemes. In these two ways the Act improved the existing situation. In two other respects, however, the Act worsened the situation of council tenants. It required that all council rents should be raised to a commercially economic level with the result that it vastly increased the number of tenants subject to a means test for rent rebates. Apart from ideological objections to the extension of means testing, there is also the very real problem of low take-up rates of means tested benefits. Second, the Act ensured that the subsidy given to council tenants came from other council tenants and that where the local authority's housing revenue was in surplus, council tenants paid towards the rent rebates of tenants in the private housing sector. The Act did nothing to alter the position of the owner-occupier but it has extended rent rebates to tenants in private accommodation. Means testing has thus become a central feature of housing policy. Reviewing the last Conservative government's plans for housing in the 1970s, Klein rightly concludes that 'policy has been reverting somewhat to the view of housing as a market commodity, with public intervention concerned more with helping people to compete in the market than with offering them public provision instead'.[38]

Housing policy has achieved some of its aims. Nationally the quality of housing has improved and in many areas shortages have disappeared. In certain areas acute shortages remain with little hope of their elimination in the foreseeable future. The same is true of unsatisfactory housing. Choice for most people is nonexistent. The distribution of subsidies remains inequitable. Exorbitant profits are being made in land speculation and in house building. Fundamentally, a family's housing reflects its economic standing rather than its needs and it will remain so until housing is treated as a social service rather than a profit-making enterprise.

Why the failure?

Why is it that in these four areas fundamental aims have not been achieved? Why have geographical inequalities in the provision of health care survived so vigorously when they stand as a denial of fundamental aims of the service? Why has poverty survived the good intentions of the post-war years and thirty years of increasing affluence? How is it that inequality of opportunity remains the most striking characteristic of the English educational system? Why are homelessness and bad housing so shockingly prevalent? The commonest explanations are in terms of shortages of resources — staff, finance or buildings. Or alternatively, failure is explained in terms of the weaknesses of policies which were basically sound in conception but had technical failings, or which faltered in execution because of 'administrative weaknesses' — the weaknesses of the central authority and the strength of local or regional authorities, or alternatively the strength of the central authority and the weaknesses of local authorities. In a society obsessed by educational credentials, lack of training for staff is another popular explanation.

Such explanations may be relevant, and they may explain specific failures of particular policies. All services always need more staff, more

117

resources, more training, better management skills, a more stream-lined administrative structure and so on. There is always more that can, and could, be done. In our view, however, such explanations are super-ficial. They might explain casual, occasional and limited failures but when used as explanations for fundamental failure to achieve central objectives they lack basic credibility. They are symbols and evidence of the way in which those concerned with social policy have abstracted the subject from the economic, social and political context in which it operates. If social policy is seen in this light, explanations for its failure will naturally be sought in terms of weaknesses and failings within services. There will always be such failings, and they are an interesting and valuable area for study and research. If, however, we set the welfare system in the economic, political and social context of an advanced capitalist economy, we can see other and, we would argue, more fundamental reasons for the failure of social policies to achieve their aims.

If it is to flourish, any economic system both requires and generates a particular value system. Capitalism is no exception. It depends on and fosters the development of an ethic of self-help, freedom, individualism, competition and achievement — the classic liberal values.

Such a value system, which is required for the successful operation of a capitalist economy, is in clear opposition to the values needed to underpin a successful public welfare system. If such a system is to flourish, the stress on the virtue of self-help must be replaced by stress on the need to help others. Individualism must be replaced by a concern for the community at large; competition by co-operation; achievement must be defined in social and communal rather than in individual terms — values which are socialist rather than liberal. The economic system and the welfare system, therefore, require and depend on quite different value systems. Conflict between economic and social purposes and between liberal and socialist values is therefore inherent in capitalist society. Wilensky and Lebeaux describe America's response to the human problems of industrialism as 'a constantly moving compromise between the values of security and humanitarianism on the one hand, and individual initiative and self reliance in the compet-itive order on the other'.[39] This captures the heart of the problem.

To grasp this value conflict is essential to an understanding of the development of social policy and to an understanding of why funda-mental aims set out in a period of post-war collectivist euphoria have not been achieved. To illustrate this thesis we consider how the key liberal values of freedom, individualism and inequality have affected social policy development.

Both the liberal and the socialist notions of freedom are reflected in social policy. The introduction of government programmes in, for example, the fields of education, health, housing and social security, financed from general taxation with or without compulsory individual contributions represents a departure from the classic liberal view of the role and function of government. Nevertheless, the framing and implementation of social policy are often subordinated to residual liberal ideas about freedom as the absence of restraint.

We take various examples of the way in which such ideas undermine the expressed aims of social policies. The success of many policies — e.g. in health, education and the personal social services — depends on securing adequate numbers of skilled staff in all areas. Such staff are nearly always in short supply. Thus a real test of the seriousness of government commitment arises. Is greater emphasis to be given to the health, education and personal social service needs of remote or unattractive areas, or is greater emphasis to be given to the freedom of workers trained at public expense to go where they prefer?

With some groups — e.g. social workers — no attempt at all is made by government to encourage or compel them to take up employment in areas of greatest need. With other groups, there are controls and incentives of varying degrees of effectiveness. General Practitioners can be refused permission by government to establish themselves in certain areas, or they can be offered financial inducements to work in deprived areas, but they cannot be directed by governments to operate in areas where their services are most needed. The Department of Education and Science, and its predecessor, the Ministry of Education, has for many years operated a quota scheme to try and ensure a fairer distribution of teachers between desirable and less desirable local education authorities. The quota, however, is no more than a gentlemanly agreement which the DES has no power to enforce. In the autumn and winter of 1973-4, when Inner London's shortage of teachers was making headlines in the national press, sixty-nine LEAs were employing more than their quota of teachers.[40] Teachers' freedom of movement was apparently judged to be more important ultimately than the education of children in London. There are, of course, some incentives aimed at encouraging teachers to work in areas of particular need — the extra payment for those who work in EPA schools and the London allowances for example. But the sums involved are less than compelling as if those responsible considered such interference with the 'natural' distribution of manpower as highly dubious.

A second area where individual freedom of staff is considered more important than the needs of services is the way in which doctors, teachers and other key workers, who have been trained at public expense, are allowed to emigrate or to practise their skills in the private sector to their greater personal profit and to the loss of the community which has financed their training. We may recoil with horror from the

119

idea of directing staff to areas of greatest need, or of restricting emigration, or of compelling those who have been trained at public expense to practise their skills for a time at least in the public sector. Such restrictions on freedom are unattractive but so too is the plight of areas desperately short of teachers, doctors, dentists and social workers. It is not only the freedom of the individual which is at stake in such debates — though this is usually what receives most attention. Also at stake is the quality of life of many people in many areas. Is it totally out of the question that individuals trained at public expense should, with proper safeguards, be sent for a time at least to areas of greatest need? Our individualistic, freedom-centred philosophy makes us emphasise the restriction on the individual, rather than the loss to the community which arises from individual freedom.

Third, governments uphold individual freedom by allowing individuals to make use of private instead of public services even when by so doing they hinder the basic aims of relevant statutory social policies. The development of private occupation welfare services, said Titmuss, comes into conflict with 'the aims and unity of social policy; for in effect, whatever their aims may be, their whole tendency at present is to divide loyalties, to nourish privilege and to narrow the social conscience.'[41] Thus, though parents are compelled to educate their children, they are not compelled to send them to State schools. Private schools are permitted to continue, partly at least to safeguard the freedom of choice of that small minority of parents who can afford to choose. In many parts of England, central and local government undermines the success of new schemes of comprehensive schooling by allowing parents to retain freedom of choice and send their children to private and State selective schools. So sacred is freedom, it seems, that the majority must suffer lest a minority should feel unfree.

Fourth, although there are occasions when the State does interfere with the freedom of individuals to do what they will with their own, attitudes to such action are highly ambivalent. One obvious example of such interference is legislation to control rents and to provide tenants with a degree of security of tenure. The ambivalence of attitudes to such legislation is, however, clear in the sentences passed by the courts on landlords found guilty of harassment or illegal eviction. Greve notes that out of over 700 convictions between the 1965 Rent Act coming into force and the end of 1969, only six resulted in imprisonment and the average fine imposed on the landlords was just under £20 — less, as was pointed out to Greve, than the cost of getting a legal eviction through the courts.[42] Clearly implicit in such light sentences is the view that such laws have a dubious moral basis and that those who offend should therefore be treated tenderly.

Another example of how liberal notions of freedom have helped perpetuate social problems and undermine the success of social policies is the failure to organise the building industry for social ends, to leave it to respond to demand rather than to organise it for the meeting of need. In a market economy builders devote their energies and resources to what promises the most profit. If this freedom is permitted then at the same time the housing problem is perpetuated. Successive governments have produced housing policies designed to solve the problems but none have sought to organise the building industry to that end. Market freedom was considered — implicitly or explicitly — more important than housing need.

The development of social policy may seem like a victory for socialist views of freedom over classical liberal thinking. This is clearly an oversimplified view. Classical liberal freedom remains a strong continuing element, explicitly and implicitly, in social policy legislation. Where the needs of particular policies conflict with classical views of freedom, freedom frequently wins. Generalised intentions about securing equality of access to medical or educational facilities or securing security of tenure to private tenants come to grief therefore on the rocks of liberal freedom.

An even stronger influence on social policy than freedom is individualism. 'In Britain', says Pinker, 'there remain deep value conflicts regarding the proper relationship between the individual and the community. Our legally extensive range of public social services derives from collectivist ideologies. At the same time, the ideology of self help and individualism receives powerful support from the continuing dominance of market values in our lives.'[43] The continuing strength of individualism is reflected in social policy in two ways in particular — in the stress on policies of self-support and on the provision of services and benefits at a minimum level. In a splendid expression of individualism the recent Conservative White Paper, 'Strategy for Pensions', declared that 'It is by personal enterprise and foresight and not by reliance on an ever widening extension of state commitments that better living standards for our people in the later years of life will be secured.'[44]

Social security systems vary from country to country in the emphasis given to the insurance-contributory element. In some countries, e.g. the USA, the stress is very much on the insurance principle and the contractual nature of the relationship into which the individual has entered. 'The emphasis on relating benefits to a contributory contractual basis, which precludes financing from general revenue', says Rimlinger, 'is an outstanding manifestation of the traditional ideals of self-help and independence carried over into a governmental "mutual help" program.'[45] In other countries, e.g. New Zealand, the social security system is financed by progressive taxation. In England the basis of the system (until April 1975) was still the flat rate insurance contribution. The result is a low level of benefits financed by regressive taxation. The history of the insurance principle since 1911, says Pinker, 'exemplifies the continuing dominance of market criteria in those major English social services concerned with income maintenance.'[46] Such insurance based systems reflect and reinforce individualism. Their basis is a stress on individual rights whereas what is vital if poverty is to be abolished is a recognition not of individual rights but of an individual's social rights. The British system manages very effectively, but quite incorrectly, to give beneficiaries the impression that they have earned through contributions the benefits which they draw and that such benefits are somehow more eligible than those financed from taxation. In fact, of course, the only difference is that those financed from taxation are financed rather less unfairly than those financed from contributions.

If we look at the Family Incomes Supplement we see what happens when there is a conflict between the proven needs of the individual and the assumed needs of the economic system to emphasise the responsibility of individuals to fend self-helpfully for themselves and their dependants. The Family Incomes Supplement is a break with the view that a family's economic position should be determined by its main breadwinner's earning capacity with the help of Family Allowances. It seeks to supplement the incomes of those whose earnings fall below a prescribed level. In this, welfare considerations temper liberal individualism. But the help that may be given is only half the difference between the family's gross income and the prescribed amount, up to a limited maximum. Poverty is eased and consciences are quietened, individual responsibility is a little bruised but survives fundamentally strong and healthy and work incentives survive only a little dimmed. Welfare considerations temper individualism — but only slightly, and poverty remains.

Stress on self-support means that the situation of those not at work must always be less eligible than the situation of those at work. The result of this philosophy is the wages stop and a low level of benefits lest incentives to work be weakened. Where many who work are in poverty then poverty must be the lot of those who cannot work — or else justice is offended.

The influence of individualism is seen very clearly in our response to the problem of poverty. The individualist response is a proliferation of means tested benefits each designed to deal with one particular facet of an individual's total problem. There is neither an overall approach to the individual's problem nor any real recognition that the faults lie not in the individual but in the system. Our individualism prevents us from correctly locating the causes of the problem or from facing the problem squarely. Because of our conception of the problem we go for solutions which are piecemeal, personal and inadequate.

Second, in addition to its expression through stress on self-support, individualism is also expressed in social policy in the nonprovision of benefits or services or in provision of benefits at a very basic, minimum level on stringent conditions. The reasons for this are two-fold. First, there is the fear that more generous benefits would undermine individual responsibility; second, there is the firm belief that benefits above the minimum are the responsibility of the individual, not of society. The result 'leaves the claims of social need subordinate to those of the economic market.'[47]

These attitudes are most obvious in social security and in housing because these services encroach most nearly on the sacred reserved areas of the market. The Beveridge Report, for example, argued that Family Allowances should meet only part of the cost of the physical maintenance of children – and not for the first child – for if the State met the full cost it would undermine the principle of parental responsibility for children. This principle found a more eager acceptance in the corridors of power than some of the others which Beveridge enunciated. It perhaps explains the way in which Family Allowances have been largely ignored by successive governments so that in 1974 they form a smaller proportion of the average earnings of male manual workers than they did in 1948. It helps explain too how provision of adequate and sufficient housing has never been clearly accepted as a responsibility of government.

A liberal individualism, then, underlies our inadequate investment in children. In its turn this helps undermine the good intentions of other social policies such as education. It can be argued that increased direct financial investment in children through higher Family Allowances or a much wider provision of school maintenance grants for 16-18 year-olds is a prerequisite of equality of opportunity. For ideological reasons we limit such investment. The result is a poorer return on expenditure in education than society might otherwise receive. Margaret Wynn has argued very forcefully that we must see the early leaving of high ability children as 'a consequence of the inadequacy of the total investment in these children by home and school'.[48]

As we have seen in chapter 3, Beveridge argued very firmly that the level of flat rate insurance benefits should be fixed to provide only for physical subsistence. If individuals wanted to make more generous provision, then they should do so privately. The State, he argued, had no responsibility beyond the guaranteeing of a minimum. Leaving such extra responsibility with individuals gave scope to 'the duty and pleasure of thrift'.[49] The fact that many individuals were clearly in no position to provide privately did not lead Beveridge to question the excellence of the principle. Such an approach has its roots in individualism and while giving scope to 'the duty and pleasure of thrift' it also perpetuates poverty.

This leads us to the third main effect which a philosophy of individualism has in the field of social welfare. That is its effect on the recipients. There is a fundamental conflict between the driving ethic of the market — competitive individualism — and the attitudes required to assert a right to welfare — a belief in co-operative rights of citizenship. For most people, Pinker argues, 'the idea of participant citizenship in distributive processes outside the market place has very little meaning. Consequently, most applicants for social services remain paupers at heart.'[50] If the market system is to survive and flourish, people must accept a competitive-individualist ethic. They must strive self-helpfully to outdo and outconsume their neighbours. People must be socialised to feel that dependence is less creditable than independence, that no system of distribution is acceptable except the market. The result of this is that 'the objective reality of the welfare state is subjectively meaningless' to many or most users. The words 'social rights' may be on the lips of the tender minded intellectuals and administrators but they are seldom in the minds of would-be beneficiaries. In practice this helps to contribute towards a low take-up of benefits and so to the perpetuation of need and inequality.

The attitudes of recipients and would-be recipients are also affected by the stigmatising procedures which are a corollary of liberal capitalist values. The wider society sees need and dependence as shameful because they are the product of individual failure. The person who is needy or dependent feels the same. Such attitudes lead inevitably to certain patterns of organisation and administration which are implicitly or overtly stigmatising. In a capitalist system such procedures are necessary, inevitable and functional. They are necessary to reinforce the value system on which capitalism depends. They are inevitable in a system where capitalism flourishes. They are functional in that through collective action, individualist goals and values are reinforced. The fundamental problem is expressed and exacerbated by complex and incomprehensible application forms, the public squalor with which such procedures are associated and the attitudes of those whose misfortune it is to represent to the needy society's inability to reconcile its value conflicts.

Stress on the ethic of individualism is an important element in the concept of income in capitalist society. Income is seen as personal and private, the reward for the private efforts of the individual, the mark of his worth and value, his to use for what he will. Such emphasis accords well with the needs of a mass producing private consumption economy but it accords very ill with the need to socialise an increasing proportion of the national income for social purposes. 'It seems a fundamental defect of our society', writes Raymond Williams, 'that social purposes are largely financed out of individual incomes, by a method of rates and taxes which makes it very easy for us to feel that society is a thing that continually deprives and limits us — without this system we could all be profitably spending . . . We can hardly have any conception, in our present system, of the financing of social purposes from the social product.'[51] In such a system public, communal expenditure is seen as a taking of resources from their natural, rightful owners and purposes to unnatural and less legitimate ends. In a capitalist system taxation must inevitably be regarded as a burden — with all the limitations on desirable and necessary public expenditure which this brings. It also leads to the view that redistribution of income — or an increase in public spending — can only be achieved at a time of economic growth when private and public spending can increase painlessly and simultaneously.

The ethic of individualism is at the heart of the problems of welfare capitalism. Individualism and welfarism live, at best, in an uneasy truce situation, at worst, in open warfare. So far, individualism has clearly been the winner in most conflicts. Its significance, however, has been its pervasiveness and the way it has continually prevented the achievement of supposed social goals. Romanyshyn has this to say of its influence in the United States. 'We have sought', he says, 'to alleviate poverty without reducing the incentive to work; to socialise the poor into a work culture in a society that has never guaranteed full employment; to strengthen family life without providing parents with essential supporting resources; to assure the "rights of childhood" without disturbing the market allocation of income, housing and medical care.'[52] Such strictures can be applied with a substantial measure of truth to this country too. They help illuminate the conflict inherent in the co-existence of the individualist ethic of capitalism and the social ethic of welfare.

In spite of its marked influence on social policy, individualism has not been an explicit warring point between liberals and socialists, between the values of capitalism and the ethic of welfare. It is in their emphasis on equality and inequality that the two value systems have seemed to differ most in the past. 'The aim of welfare services', Marshall points out, 'is to give equal care to similar cases. "Capitalism" — or the market — lives by recognising and rewarding inequalities and depends on them to provide the motive force that makes it work.'[53] As with the other two social values discussed above it is, on the whole, liberal-capitalist rather than socialist-welfare attitudes to equality, that have been dominant in the field of social policy. First, social policy has been concerned essentially with modifying inequality rather than with achieving equality. An additional, allied, limitation is that social policy has been concerned only with certain limited kinds of inequality, not with inequality in general. Its concern has been confined to inequalities when their continuance would have been dysfunctional economically, socially, politically or militarily. The social policy areas where most stress has been laid on equality are health and education. Continuing gross inequalities of access to health care and education were clearly dysfunctional. Another important factor is that inequalities in these areas could be modified without a substantial challenge to the free market system, whereas a modification of the distribution of income provides a much more direct and immediate challenge.

Second, when social policy has been concerned with equality the concern has been with equality of opportunity, rather than equality of outcome. But as Tawney pointed out, forty years ago, the existence of equality of opportunity 'depends not merely on the absence of disabilities, but on the presence of abilities.'[54] After thirty years of supposed equality of opportunity in education, the hollowness of the slogan has been fully exposed.

A third issue which throws light on the influence of liberal attitudes to equality on social policy is that of Educational Priority Areas and positive discrimination. The Plowden Committee concluded that equality of opportunity could only be achieved by giving some children an unequally generous chance — that giving children the same opportunity simply confirmed existing inequalities — so that discrimination was a prerequisite of equality.[55] The scanty support and resources given to EPAs by both Labour and Conservative governments show the weakness of the commitment to equality. One commentator has remarked that the problem with EPAs is that equality has an appealing ring, whereas discrimination does not. This is true, but the appeal of equality is apparently not strong enough to encourage governments to experiment with policies which might go some way at least towards making a reality of the entirely liberal notion of equality of opportunity.

Fourth, the continuing and almost unchanged inequalities of wealth and income show how limited and partial is public concern for equality. Essentially, social policy is concerned with horizontal redistribution of income — from young to old, from the childless to those with children, from the employed to the unemployed, from the healthy to the sick — rather than with the more egalitarian vertical redistribution from better off to worse off. In Webb and Sieve's words, social policy is concerned with 'contingency redistribution' rather than with 'income redistribution'.[56]

The illusion of an egalitarian and almost confiscatory tax system is preserved by seemingly high rates of taxation. The reality is, however, rather less frightening. Rates of taxation may be high but their burden is eased by allowances and exemptions. In 1971-2, specific tax reliefs on occupational pensions, mortgage interest, child tax allowances and life assurance eased the burden on the taxpayer to the extent of some £2,500m.[57] The heavier the supposed tax burden on individuals, the greater the concessions and the benefits. So inequality is preserved together with the illusion of egalitarian policies.

Similarly, the present levels of estate duty seem to involve very high rates of taxation on wealth at the death of its owner. But legislation is so lacking in conviction that it offers simple exemptions of which all but the utterly stupid and misanthropic sensibly take advantage. Death duties are for the better off scarcely more than voluntary. The whole procedure, as Henry Simons said of the American tax system, 'involves a subtle kind of moral and political dishonesty . . . the politician may point with pride to the rates, while reminding their wealthy constituents of the loopholes.'[58]

The non-egalitarian ethic of our tax system is implicit too in the amount of revenue raised by non-progressive taxation. Taxes on expenditure, national insurance contributions and local rates are far more important as a source of revenue than income tax. According to popular belief, the tax system in Britain is progressive. In fact, as Kincaid points out, 'The British tax system is on the whole a non-progressive one. The higher income groups certainly hand over more money in taxation but as a proportion of income the incidence of taxation remains pretty even over a very wide bank of income from poor to rich.'[59]

Finally, in spite of a supposed concern with equality, governments allow the continuance of social policy measures which support and buttress inequalitites. Meacher compares the figures quoted above on public expenditure on private welfare (i.e. tax concessions) in 1971-2 with the £900m. from public funds spent on the Exchequer supplement to state retirement pensions, local authority rent subsidies and family allowances.[60] Government subsidies to private welfare provision of this kind clearly buttress and often increase inequality. The same could be argued in relation to private medicine and private education, both of which are subsidised in various ways from public funds. Such policies allow the better off to maintain and consolidate their position. If expenditure on private schooling increases the chance of successful entry to university, it increases the chance of a massive subsidy from public funds even to the most affluent parent who pays only about one-third of the true cost of a university place. Such a place in turn increases future earning power and helps maintain inequality.

Social policies aimed at increasing equality have failed for a number of reasons. The most important reason is that they run counter to the classic liberal values and when there is conflict, liberal values seem to triumph. Equality of opportunity in education is seldom taken to imply that the better off should be prevented from purchasing unequally generous educational opportunities in the private sector. Such is our concern for freedom that such a legitimate interpretation of the popular slogan hardly crosses our minds. Yet if we accept the slogan, the abolition of inferior and superior opportunities should surely go together. Similarly, egalitarian systems of taxation are modified so that individual entrepreneurs can be adequately rewarded for initiative and enterprise. Again, those who are able self-helpfully to save for retirement or house purchase must be encouraged to do so and duly rewarded. Because of our belief that individuals have a right to hand on to their heirs and assigns any wealth they may have accumulated, we provide a wide range of escape routes from seemingly high rates of estate duty. The imposition of high rates of tax is the product of our belief in equality but the more detailed regulations and arrangements reflect our stronger belief in freedom and individualism.

When attempted more vigorously, egalitarian social policies − as in education − have foundered on the realities of the social and economic system. An unequal society means quite simply that different social groups are differentially equipped to make use of opportunities. Offering the same opportunities simply perpetuates inequalitites. Freedom and individualism fit well with a belief in equality of opportunity, less well with the kind of policies such as positive discrimination, which might make a reality of such beliefs.

We have looked at each social value and its influence on social policy separately for discussion purposes. In real life, these and other values act on and interact with each other and they resist and reinforce political, social, economic and other factors. It is not, however, a completely chaotic and unpredictable picture. In this conflict and interaction between social values, those values that are functional to the existing social and economic system and hence to the interests of the dominant classes tend to prevail, even if in a diluted form. No one can claim that the classical liberal values of freedom, individualism and inequality have not undergone substantial modificaton during the past century. The central values of the welfare state represent an uneasy compromise between the classical and socialist conception of such values, though still weighted in favour of the liberal tradition.

Social values are not unconnected with the class structure of society. They are functional to the existing capitalist system and hence to the economic interests of the dominant social classes. It is in this way that one can claim that social values and economic interests have been the two main determinants of social policy. Other factors such as administrative structure, personnel, new knowledge, etc., are also important but they are of a different, of a secondary nature. Whichever field of social policy one looks at, it is true to say that the initial high expectations generated in the euphoria of the immediate post second world war years have at best not been completely fulfilled and at worst have remained largely unfulfilled. Though much has been achieved, a great deal has not. The pattern has been uneven with the least progress in areas of policy where economic interests are central. Welfare capitalism has modified the excesses of laissez-faire capitalism but it has not fulfilled the abstract egalitarian aims of social policies. Moreover, the experience of the last thirty years shows that there is no inherent tendency in social policy to produce a socially just society.

The basis for a new beginning

We see the conflict between the values of capitalism and the ethic of welfare as the underlying reason for the failure of social policies to achieve agreed aims. The thrust of welfare policy has been hopelessly weakened because of the absence of a set of values which support and legitimate welfare policy. Essentially, social policies have been grafted on to an economic system intrinsically hostile to the welfare ethic. In this last brief section we set out by way of conclusion a value basis for a new radical social policy.

Equality has so far acted as the main inspiration to all left wing radicals. Tawney, Laski, Crosland, Titmuss, Miliband and Strachey differ on many points but they agree on one fundamental issue: they aspire to a more egalitarian society. There are many brands of equality. This is why it has united such diverse socialist thinkers. The brand that has been incorporated in social policy is equality of opportunity, i.e. the belief that every individual has a right to such services and circumstances as will enable him to fulfil his abilities. This is a meritocratic view of equality. The emphasis is on equality of competition rather than equality of results. It is the direct offspring of individualism humanised by the efforts of the welfare state. As such it is the product of a constellation of values that represents a compromise between laissez-faire and equality of results. It is a step forward from nineteenth-century philosophy because it accepts and welcomes government intervention and because it makes for a society stratified on the basis of achievement rather than ascription.

The period since the end of the last war has made quality of opportunity the central value of social policy. Educational policies, particularly, were shaped to enable every child to compete with other children on an equal footing. If the educational race was fair then the outcome of the race was also fair, it was argued. In recent years, however, equality of opportunity has been losing its attraction as evidence has accumulated that egalitarian policies in fact produce inegalitarian results. Increasingly, it has come to be accepted that equality of opportunity is unattainable in an unequal society. Radicals too have accepted that equality of opportunity in an unequal society does not produce greater equality. It simply produces different inequalities which to the true egalitarian are not much less objectionable than those they have replaced.

This realisation has led radicals to a re-examination of their position. It has led them to a search for a new interpretation of equality. Jencks's work reflects this change of mood. The available evidence on educational achievement in the United States led him and his associates to reach two important conclusions. The first was non-controversial because it was a re-affirmation of what was already generally known. It referred to the bias of the educational system in favour of the middle and upper classes and concluded that this was a self-reinforcing relationship which could not be changed by educational policies such as positive discrimination. The second conclusion was far more important because it was new and because it had very important implications. He found little relationship between a person's educational achievement on one hand and his occupation, income and job satisfaction on the other. The fact that no such statistical relationship was established does not, of course, mean that it does not exist. Nevertheless, even with this qualification, Jencks's conclusion is most important for social policy discussions.

As a result of these findings Jencks argues that radicals must alter the nature of their demands with regard to equality.[61]

> Instead of trying to reduce people's capacity to gain a competitive advantage on one another, we would have to change the rules of the game so as to reduce the rewards of competitive success and the costs of failure. Instead of trying to make everyone equally lucky or equally good at his job, we would have to devise 'insurance' systems which neutralize the effects of luck, and income-sharing systems which break the link between vocational success and living standards.

In essence, this is a plea for social policy to switch its concern from equality of opportunity to equality of result. We must be concerned not with equalising access to the steps up the pyramid of income distribution but with altering the shape of the pyramid — with, to use Marshall's metaphor, converting the skyscraper into a bungalow.

One of the main weaknesses of egalitarian demands over the years has been that the general public has not shown much enthusiasm for substantive income equality. While inequality has been legitimated by the values of individualism and equality of opportunity, equality on the other hand has lacked a justifying value framework that would appeal to the public. Recent work on the nature of social justice has, we believe, provided a possible basis for a new and more vigorous egalitarianism. Concern with the outcomes of policy inevitably leads to a broader concern with the nature of society, its goals and ends, whereas concern for equality of opportunity restricts concern to the mechanics of the social and economic system.

Runciman's and Rawls's writings are the latest major contribution to the new thinking on social justice. 'Justice is the first virtue of social institutions', writes Rawls, 'as truth is of systems of thought. A theory, however elegant and economical must be rejected or revised if it is untrue; likewise laws and institutions no matter how efficient and well-arranged must be reformed or abolished if they are unjust.'[62] Thus, according to Rawls, justice is the central social value by which not only social policy but society in general must be guided. The general principle of justice is the 'difference principle': 'All social primary goods — liberty and opportunity, income and wealth, and the bases of self-respect — are to be distributed equally unless an unequal distribution of any or all of these goods is to the advantage of the least favored.'[63] Equality, in other words, is the fundamental social principle and inequalities have to be justified according to criteria that are compatible with justice and which help the disadvantaged members of society.

The distribution of national resources according to social justice is more in line with the wishes of free and rational men in an initial position of equality than is distribution according to a competitive inequality. People in an initial position of equality, argues Rawls, would reject the principle of utility and 'would choose two rather different principles: the first requires equality in the assignment of basic rights and duties, while the second holds that social and economic inequalities, for example inequalities of wealth and authority, are just only if they result in compensating benefits for everyone, and in particular for the least advantaged members of society.'[64] People would vote for the difference principle because, without knowing in advance their own talents and position in the social structure, they would consider this a fairer way of arranging human relationships. Though inequalities will exist in a just society they will be subject to the strictest of tests. 'The test of inequalities', says Runciman, 'is whether they can be justified to the losers; and for the winners to be able to do this, they must be prepared, in principle, to change places.'[65]

The satisfaction of need is the primary aim of the difference principle of social justice. The motto of a socially just society is, generally speaking, 'from each according to his abilities, to each according to his needs'. Thus Rawls explains that the difference principle has two important implications for public policy. The first is that natural talents are a social asset to be used primarily for the benefit of the community. The difference principle, he writes,[66]

> represents, in effect, an agreement to regard the distribution of natural talents as a common asset and to share in the benefits of this distribution whatever it turns out to be. Those who have been favored by nature, whoever they are, may gain from their good fortune only on terms that improve the situation of those who have lost out.

Second, not only are the most able to use their talents to the benefit of the community but public policy must provide more resources for the less gifted to enable them to be as equal compared to the rest of society as possible. This is the principle of redress, i.e.[67]

> the principle that undeserved inequalities call for redress; and since inequalities of birth and natural endowment are undeserved, these inequalities are to be somehow compensated for. Thus, the principle holds that in order to treat all persons equally, to provide genuine equality of opportunity, society must give more attention to those with fewer native assets and to those born into the less favorable social positions. The idea is to redress the bias of contingencies in the direction of equality. In pursuit of this principle greater resources might be spent on the education of the less rather than the more intelligent, at least over a certain time of life, say the earlier years of school.

Thus the twin principles of communal use of natural ability and of redress, both of which flow from the genuine difference principle, are ethical justifications for public policy measures that meet people's needs and hence equalise resources among individuals of equal needs. The priority given to the satisfaction of needs is justified by the contractual model of free and rational men seeking their own interests in an initial state of equality. In other words, rational men, in a state of equality and in ignorance of their future, are likely to agree that the nation's resources should be used to satisfy people's needs before being used for anything else. After all, they could find themselves in a situation where, though their own basic needs are not met, public resources are being used to satisfy other people's whims.

The satisfaction of needs would mean a socially just but unequal distribution of resources because people's needs can vary. The needs of the retarded child are greater than the needs of the normal child; those of the disabled are greater than those of the physically fit; those of the married man with two children are greater than those with one or no children, and so on. This difference in needs, however, need not be exaggerated. It has to be assumed that people's needs are the same unless a case to the contrary is established. While it is true that people's needs can vary, it is even more true that people's needs do not vary all that much.

In addition to need, Runciman suggests two other criteria for the distribution of income — merit and contribution to the common good. We will argue that need should be the only criterion for social services while the other two criteria should be used in the case of income from work.

All these criteria present two inter-related problems for social policy purposes: how to define needs and how to measure them. One way of defining needs is to plot them on a continuum ranging from those 'basic' needs which are needed for physical survival — food, housing, clothing and heating — at one end of the continuum, to those which are relative in the middle of the continuum — cars, the theatre, holidays, etc., and to those which are luxuries at the other end of the continuum — yachting, champagne, fur coats, etc. There are two fundamental difficulties with this categorisation: first, it is not always possible to agree where to place a need on the continuum, particularly those needs falling between relative needs and luxuries. Second, though a distinction can be made between basic needs on one hand and other needs on the other, the distinction is obscured by the fact that basic needs are defined in a relative way. To complicate the issue even more, relative needs can become basic needs for some people. Holidays, for example, are a relative need, generally speaking, but for people who work under great pressure a break from work may be as necessary to their health as adequate clothing. We are led to the inescapable conclusion that all needs are relative but some are more relative than others.

The question of measurement of needs is as complicated as the definition of needs for the two overlap. Basically, there are two approaches to the measurement of need — the populist and the expert approach. The populist approach relies on the public's views as to what needs are. What people want is defined as need. Bradshaw refers to two inadequacies of this approach: first, such 'felt need' 'is limited by the perceptions of the individual'; and second, 'it is thought to be inflated by those who ask for help without "really needing it".'[68] Another basic weakness of this approach is to decide what constitutes 'the public'. In the case of needs such as food, which apply to the general population, does one accept the opinion of the majority, and, if so, what constitutes majority? In the case of sectional needs such as meals on wheels for the elderly, do we rely on the opinions of the potential consumers or on the opinion of the general public? In spite of these criticisms, the concept of felt need is fundamental to the identification and measurement of needs for social policy purposes. 'If it is a tenet of democracy that people take as much responsibility for their own lives and community aspects of living as possible,' comments Walton, 'it follows that the concept of "felt need" must be introduced.'[69] Nevertheless, the concept of felt need suffers from two basic weaknesses: first, people do not always know what they need and second, the limited social horizons of the lower income groups restrict their demands.

The expert approach relies on the views of the professionals in a particular field for the identification and measurement of relevant needs. At the level of social policy planning, it can be in agreement as well as in opposition to the populist view of need. The twin criticisms of felt need indicate that the expert approach to need can act both as a force for raising as well as for lowering the standard of need. Architects and town planners as a profession may set housing standards which in some ways are higher and in others lower than the public demands. The teaching profession's views of what are educational needs and how they should be met can be very different from what the public, whether children or their parents, consider to be appropriate. The weaknesses of the expert approach to need are as fundamental as those of the populist approach. Professional groups are motivated by self- interest as well as altruism. They are also elitist groups, constituent parts of the establishment and their assessment of need must, almost inevitably, be such as to leave the overall socio-economic structure of society unaltered. Finally, there is not always agreement even among the differing professionals in a particular area about what the appropriate standards of need are at any one time, apart from the equally difficult issue of who are the relevant professionals in a particular area of need. In spite of these difficulties, the expert approach to the measurement of need is indispensable to social policy making, for experts possess knowledge not available to other population groups.

Both the populist and the expert view of how to measure need are influenced by the prevailing relevant standards in society. It is in this way that a third means of measuring need — the comparative approach — presents itself. In other words, to decide what the needs of a particular group are, one looks at the relevant levels of expenditure or consumption in the rest of society. Again there are immense difficulties. If one wants to decide what, let us say, the food needs of the elderly are, which other population group does one use for comparative purposes? The rest of society? The higher income groups? The lower income groups? Or the average income group? Nevertheless, the comparative approach has the merit of acknowledging openly that there are few scientific answers to the question of need determination. Moreover, as Forder points out, the comparative approach 'can represent a particularly radical approach to the concept of need' if it uses the higher income groups as its reference point. [70]

All three approaches to the measurement of needs are necessary for social policy purposes. In the past, far too much weight has been given by governments to professional opinion and far too little to public opinion. Also, when the comparative approach has been used it has tended to make use of the standard of living of lower income groups as its reference point. There is no one answer as to which method is the best for the determination of need. Indeed, the approach one uses will depend on views of what the just distribution of goods in society should be. We agree with Harvey's verdict that 'We must select among the various methods for determining need in such a way that we maximize on the social justice of the result.' [71]

Need is the basic criterion for the allocation of income in a socially just society. Nevertheless, it cannot be the only one in an affluent society where the national income is abundant enough to satisfy definable needs with a surplus still remaining. This surplus can be allocated in one of two ways: either equally to every citizen or according to the two criteria of merit and contribution to the common good which were suggested earlier. It appears to be more in line with the principle of social justice to allocate this surplus according to these two criteria than simply in an equal way to all. Rational men in an initial state of equality would probably agree that, when socially defined needs have been met, any surplus of national income should be distributed according to these two criteria rather than be distributed equally.

Both criteria are difficult to define — perhaps more difficult than need. Merit refers predominantly to the difficulty of the work done, the danger involved in the work and the skill required. Contribution to the common good refers mainly to the amount and value of what is produced, the degree to which social and economic objectives are furthered and the degree to which pleasure is given and pain relieved by the particular job. Undoubtedly, these are rather vague criteria for the allocation of surplus national income but they are nevertheless more socially just than the existing criteria of power, scarcity and tradition.

We have given more space to the discussion of need than the other two criteria for need is not only the basic criterion, it is the sole criterion for the allocation of social service benefits. Moreover, we are in search of a principle rather than a detailed programme for a socially just society. As Jencks has explained, 'The first step toward redistributing income is not devising ingenious machinery for taking money from the rich and giving it to the poor, but convincing large numbers of people that this is a desirable objective.' [72] There is the need for a new ideology that can legitimise and give ethical backing for government policies that are designed to create a socially just society.

What are, then, the minimum implications of the principle of social justice for the four broad areas of social policy which we discussed earlier? In the field of income and wealth it means the abolition of wealth inheritance above a very basic amount; it also means the payment of wages primarily according to need and then according to the criterion of merit and contribution to the common good. The amount of social security benefits must be solely according to need and irrespective of such criteria as contribution conditions, previous earnings, or the other paraphernalia of insurance schemes.

As far as medical care is concerned, while the National Health Service is theoretically based on socially just criteria, changes, however, are necessary to ensure a territorially just distribution of medical resources, equality of treatment for all types of patient groups, and the abolition of all direct charges on health service consumers.

As for housing, in a socially just society, government responsibility would be total. A family's housing should not depend on ability to pay but on its needs. In spite of the difficulties involved in defining need, there is substantial agreement in theory among the policy pronouncements of the main political parties. Four criteria for minimum standards, which appear to be generally acceptable are, first, that dwellings should be fit according to the criteria defined in the Housing Act of 1957; second, that everyone should possess the four basic housing amenities i.e. internal toilet, fixed bath, hot and cold water system and wash basin; third, that housing should be in an adequate state of repair; and fourth, that an acceptable occupancy rate such as the bedroom occupancy rate used by recent government surveys should be achieved. Clearly these are minimum standards and, as we said earlier, they are changing constantly. What is currently lacking is not agreement on standards for housing needs, but government commitment to the satisfaction of these needs.

The educational system in the type of society we envisage will ensure territorial justice in the distribution of educational resources, it will lay stress on positive discrimination for disadvantaged groups and areas and it will provide better opportunities for adult education, particularly for the early school leaver.

In all the social policy areas that we have discussed, two further principles will apply. First, active participation by the general public will be a central feature of the social services. Such a policy increases public interest in the services as well as public awareness of the problems involved. Moreover, and partly as a result, the power of the professionals becomes a little trimmed and hence more responsible. Second, private provision will be illegal with the exception of housing.

In social security, health and education, universal state provision is much more likely than selective provision to be of a satisfactory standard. Housing is different from the other services in that owner occupation is already the dominant form of housing provision. It is also different in that housing is a commodity rather than a service.

A socially just society is a society where equality is the accepted principle for the distribution of resources and where inequalities have to be justified. Inequalities would exist as a result of the application of need, merit and contribution to the common good as criteria for allocating resources. In other words, inequalities would be acceptable only on the grounds of equity, of the way they benefit the generality and the way they benefit the worst off members of society.

Inequalities would be judged indefensible if they were the result of birth or inheritance; if they were simply the result of social circumstances; if they were simply the product of differences in natural abilities; if they were not to the benefit of all and if others were harmed by them. In a socially just society, prosperity and unsatisfied need would not co-exist; the needs of all would be satisfied before resources were allocated for any other purpose.

At its present stage of development the welfare state constitutes a form of capitalism. It is welfare capitalism compared to the early laissez-faire capitalism. As such, it cannot solve the fundamental social problem of the unjust inequality in income, housing, education and health facilities. The socially just society we envisage involves the redistribution of resources from the powerful sections of the community to the weak sections. Under present circumstances the possibilities of this happening either peacefully or violently appear remote. Those with most power will not willingly, and perhaps may not peacefully, give up their privileges. Those with least power neither openly claim, nor would perhaps support, a system of resource distribution based primarily on need for they are largely motivated by the values of welfare capitalism. On the other hand there is a more vigorous and persistent questioning of wide pay differentials. They are no longer treated as sacrosanct. There is general consensus that low-paid workers should be protected by governments and that poverty should be eradicated. It is, in brief, a confused and contradictory value system. The reigning ideology in social and economic policy is not as unchallenged as it was in the past.
The welfare state is clearly not the end of the road of social evolution. What will succeed it depends on such a complex variety of economic, social and political factors of a national and international scale that it makes prediction no more than crystal-ball gazing.

The fact that the prospects of a socially just society appear remote should not make it any less worth striving for. Reform may, of necessity, have to be through a stumbling incrementalism but clarity about objectives must underlie any purposeful examination of alternative policies. Too much social reform thinking has been concerned with narrow and immediate objectives and with ways and means rather than with attempting to clarify goals. In order to escape from the piecemeal pragmatism which is the characteristic of British social reform (and of social administration) we have attempted to concentrate on ends rather than on means. To do so is to expose oneself to the charge of unrealistic romanticism. Our defence is that the piecemeal social reform of the last thirty years has failed to do more than scratch the surface of social and economic inequality. Concentration on ways and means is likely to perpetuate such a situation. The only escape lies in a reconsideration of fundamental social objectives. To this process we have tried to contribute.

Notes

Introduction

1. J.K. Galbraith, 'Economics, Peace and Laughter', Houghton, Mifflin, 1971, p. 43.
2. E. M. Burns, 'Ideas in Conflict', Methuen, 1963, p. 196.
3. H. Thomas, 'John Strachey', Eyre Methuen, 1973, p. 129.

Chapter 1   Society, the State, social problems and social policy

1. The term 'order theories' is used here to include theories known in the sociological literature as order theories, consensus theories and functionalist theories. Obviously there are differences of approach and emphasis among the various sociologists of this broad school of thought but for this discussion Parsons's views only are used as they are central to this literature.
2. R. Dahrendorf, 'Class and Class Conflict in Industrial Society', Routledge & Kegan Paul, 1959, p. 161.
3. T. Parsons, 'Sociological Theory and Modern Society', Free Press, 1969, p. 6.
4. T. Parsons, 'Towards a General Theory of Action', Harvard University Press, 1951, p. 227.
5. D. Lockwood, Some Remarks on 'The Social System', 'British Journal of Sociology', vol. vii, no. 2, 1956.
6. A. W. Gouldner, 'The Coming Crisis of Western Sociology', Heinemann, 1971, p. 353.
7. P.L. Van den Berghe, Dialectic and Functionalism: Towards a Theoretical Synthesis, 'American Sociological Review', vol.28, no.5, October 1963.
8. A. Inkeles, 'What is Sociology? An Introduction to the Discipline and Profession', Prentice-Hall, 1964.
9. T. Parsons, The Distribution of Power in American Society, 'World Politics', vol. x, no. 1, October 1957.

10 J.K. Galbraith, 'American Capitalism' (1952), Penguin, 1963, p. 125.
11 R.A. Dahl, 'Who Governs?', Yale University Press, 1961, p. 216.
12 R.A. Dahl, 'Social Science Research on Business: Product and Potential', Columbia University Press, 1959, p. 36.
13 L. Perrow, The Sociological Perspective and Political Pluralism, 'Social Research', vol. 31, no. 4, Winter 1964.
14 R.A. Nisbet and R.K. Merton, 'Contemporary Social Problems', Harcourt, Brace & World, 1966, p. 804.
15 Ibid., pp. 802-3.
16 J.K. Galbraith, 'The Affluent Society', Penguin, 2nd ed., 1970, pp. 260-2.
17 W. Ryan, 'Blaming the Victim', Orbach & Chambers, 1971, p. 27.
18 Ibid., p. 7.
19 C. Kerr et al., 'Industrialism and Industrial Man', Harvard University Press, 1960.
20 D. Bell, 'The End of Ideology', Free Press, 1960, pp. 402-3.
21 T. Parsons, Communism and the West, The Sociology of the Conflict in A. and E. Etzioni (eds), 'Social Change', Basic Books, 1964, p. 397.
22 A. V. Dicey, 'Law and Public Opinion in England', Macmillan, 2nd ed., 1962, p. 22.
23 F.A. Hayek, 'The Constitution of Liberty', Routledge & Kegan Paul, 1960, p. 260.
24 J.H. Goldthorpe, The Development of Social Policy in England 1800-1914, 'Transactions of the Fifth World Congress of Sociology', vol. 4, 1962, pp. 50-1.
25 R. Dubin, Approaches to the Study of Social Conglict: A Colloquium, 'Conflict Resolution', vol. 1, no. 2, June 1957.
26 L. Coser, 'The Functions of Social Conflict', Routledge & Kegan Paul, 1956.
27 F. Parkin, 'Class Inequality and Political Order', MacGibbon & Kee, 1971, p. 81.
28 N. Birnbaum, 'The Crisis of Industrial Society', Oxford University Press, 1969, p. 5.
29 H. Marcuse, 'One-Dimensional Man', Routledge & Kegan Paul, 1964.
30 For a good essay on studies supporting the pluralist and the elitist view of power see: M. Mankoff, Power in Advanced Capitalist Society: A Review Essay, 'Social Problems', vol. 17, 1969-70.
31 C.W. Mills, 'The Power Elite', Oxford University Press, 1956.
32 T.B. Bottomore, 'Elites and Society', Pitman, 1964.
33 P. Worsley, The Distribution of Power in Industrial Society in J. Urry and J. Wakeford (eds), 'Power in Britain', Heinemann, 1973, p. 251.
34 Ibid., p. 253.
35 Birnbaum, op. cit., p. 76.
36 J.R. Rule, The Problem With Social Problems, 'Politics and Society', vol. 2, no. 1, 1971.
37 Nisbet and Merton, op. cit., p. 785.
38 R. Ross and G.L. Staines, The Politics of Analysing Social Problems, 'Social Problems', vol. 20, no.1, Summer 1972.
39 J. Horton, Order and Conflict Theories of Social Problems as Competing Ideologies, 'American Journal of Sociology', vol. 71, no. 6, May 1966.
40 G.M. Sykes, 'Social Problems in America', Scott, Foresman, 1971, pp. 9-10.
41 M. Parenti, The Possibilities for Political Change, 'Politics and Society', vol. 1, no. 1, November 1970.
42 J. Rex, 'Key Problems of Sociological Theory,' Routledge &

Kegan Paul, 1961, pp. 127-9.

Chapter 2   The anti-collectivists

1   A.V. Dicey, 'Law and Public Opinion in England', Macmillan, 2nd ed., 1962, p. 259.
2   F.A. Hayek, 'The Constitution of Liberty', Routledge & Kegan Paul, 1960, p. 11.
3   Ibid., p. 133.
4   Ibid., p. 21.
5   Ibid., p. 19.
6   M. Friedman, 'Capitalism and Freedom', University of Chicago Press, 1962, p. 2.
7   F.A. Hayek, 'Individualism and Economic Order', Routledge & Kegan Paul, 1949, p. 6.
8   Ibid., p. 6.
9   Ibid.
10   Ibid.
11   Ibid.
12   Ibid., p. 8.
13   Ibid., p. 7.
14   Ibid., p. 23.
15   Ibid., p. 22.
16   Friedman, op. cit., p. 195.
17   Hayek, 'The Constitution of Liberty', p. 91.
18   Ibid., p. 85.
19   Friedman, op. cit., p. 169.
20   Hayek, 'The Constitution of Liberty', p. 88.
21   Friedman, op. cit., p. 15.
22   Ibid., p. 121.
23   Hayek, 'The Constitution of Liberty', p. 26.
24   E. Powell, 'Freedom and Reality', Elliot Right Way Books, 1969, p. 10.
25   E. Powell, 'Still to Decide', Elliot Right Way Books, 1972, p. 12.
26   Ibid., p. 27.
27   Ibid., p. 14.
28   A. Lejeune (ed.), 'Enoch Powell', Stacey, 1970, p. 138.
29   E. Powell, 'Medicine and Politics', Pitman, 1966, p. 20.
30   Ibid., p. 16.
31   Powell, 'Still to Decide', p. 99.
32   F.A. Hayek, 'The Road to Serfdom', Routledge, 1944, p. 27.
33   Ibid., pp. 40-8.
34   F.A. Hayek, 'Law, Legislation and Liberty', vol. I, Routledge & Kegan Paul, 1973, p. 14.
35   Powell, 'Freedom and Reality', p. 10.
36   Hayek, 'The Road to Serfdom', p. 53.
37   Friedman, op. cit., p. 8.
38   Ibid., p. 16.
39   Hayek, 'The Road to Serfdom', p. 69.
40   Powell, 'Still to Decide', p. 111.
41   Friedman, op. cit., p. 34.
42   Ibid., p. 25.
43   Ibid.
44   Ibid.
45   Hayek, 'The Road to Serfdom', p. 29.

46 Lejeune, op. cit., p. 37.
47 Friedman, op. cit., p. 28.
48 Ibid., p. 29.
49 Ibid., p. 30.
50 Ibid., p. 31.
51 Ibid., p. 34.
52 Hayek, 'The Constitution of Liberty', p. 256.
53 Powell, 'Freedom and Reality', p. 8.
54 Ibid., p. 13.
55 Friedman, op. cit., p. 201.
56 Lejeune, op. cit., p. 26.
57 Ibid., p. 57.
58 Hayek, 'The Constitution of Liberty', p. 256.
59 Powell, 'Still to Decide', p. 103.
60 Lejeune, op. cit., p. 38.
61 J. Ortega y Gasset, 'History as a System and Other Essays', Norton, 1961, p. 58.
62 T. W. Hutchinson, 'Half a Century of Hobarts', Institute of Economic Affairs, 1970, p. 10.
63 Lejeune, op. cit., p. 32.
64 Hayek, 'The Constitution of Liberty', p. 344.
65 Lejeune, op. cit., p. 70.
66 Ibid.
67 Hayek, 'The Constitution of Liberty', p. 377.
68 Friedman, op. cit., p. 107.
69 Ibid., p. 192.
70 Lejeune, op. cit., p. 125.
71 Ibid., p. 124.
72 Friedman, op. cit., p. 189.
73 Lejeune, op. cit., p. 127.
74 Hayek, 'The Constitution of Liberty', p. 297.
75 Ibid., p. 298.
76 Ibid.
77 Ibid., pp. 299-300.
78 Ibid., p. 300.
79 D.S. Lees, 'Health Through Choice', Institute of Economic Affairs, 1961, p. 14.
80 Ibid., p. 14.
81 Ibid., p. 15.
82 R. Harris in 'Right Turn', ed. R. Boyson, Churchill Press, 1970, p. 17.

Chapter 3   The reluctant collectivists

1 D. Winch, 'Economics and Policy', Hodder & Stoughton, 1969, p. 221.
2 'It is not possible to draw a hard and fast line between individualism and collectivism. You cannot draw it either in theory or practice. That is where the socialist makes a mistake. Let us not imitate that mistake. No man can be a collectivist alone or an individualist alone. He must be both an individualist and a collectivist.' W.S. Churchill, 'Liberalism and the Social Problem', Hodder & Stoughton, 1909, p. 79.
3 W.H, Beveridge, 'The Pillars of Security', Macmillan (New York), 1943, p. 118.
4 J.K. Galbraith, 'The New Industrial State', Deutsch, 1967, 2nd ed.,

1972, pp. 363-4.
5   J.K. Galbraith, 'Economics and the Public Purpose', Deutsch, 1974, p. 277.
6   For an interesting recent attempt see P. Walker, The Moral Case for
     Capitalism, 'Sunday Times', 26 May 1974.
7   R.F. Harrod, 'The Life of John Maynard Keynes', Macmillan, 1951,
     pp. 331-2.
8   W.H. Beveridge, 'Full Employment in a Free Society', Allen & Unwin,
     1944, p. 19.
9   Ibid., p. 248.
10   J.K. Galbraith, 'The Affluent Society', Penguin, 2nd ed. 1970, p. 280.
11   Harrod, op. cit., p. 436.
12   Beveridge, 'Full Employment in a Free Society', p. 21.
13   Ibid., p. 36.
14   Ibid., p. 32.
15   W.H. Beveridge, 'Why I am a Liberal', Jenkins, 1945, p. 9.
16   J.M. Keynes, 'The General Theory of Employment, Interest and Money'
     (1936), Macmillan, 1946, p. 380.
17   S.E. Harris, 'John Maynard Keynes', Scribner's, 1955, p. 75; cf. H.
     Macmillan, 'The Middle Way', Macmillan, 1938, pp. 97-102.
18   W.H. Beveridge, 'Voluntary Action', Allen & Unwin, 1948, p. 320.
19   Beveridge, 'Why I am a Liberal', p. 27.
20   Harrod, op. cit., p. 333.
21   Keynes, 'The General Theory . . .', p. 374.
22   Ibid.
23   Beveridge, 'The Pillars of Security', p. 42.
24   Galbraith, 'The Affluent Society', p. 251: cf. 'Economics and the Public
     Purpose', p. 266.
25   Ibid., p. 21.
26   Ibid., p. 5.
27   Ibid., p. 98.
28   J.M. Keynes, 'The End of Laissez-Faire', Hogarth (1926), 1927, p. 39.
29   M. Stewart, 'Keynes and After', Penguin, 1967, p. 88.
30   J. Robinson, 'Economic Philosophy' (1962), Penguin, 1973, p. 73.
31   Beveridge, 'Full Employment in a Free Society', p. 29.
32   Galbraith, 'The New Industrial State', p. 225.
33   Ibid., p. 6.
34   Ibid., p. 33.
35   Galbraith, 'Economics and the Public Purpose', p. 179.
36   Galbraith, 'The New Industrial State', p. 251.
37   Ibid., p. 261.
38   Galbraith, 'Economics and the Public Purpose', pp. 190-1.
39   R,F. Harrod, Keynes the Economist, in S.E. Harris (ed.), 'The New
     Economics − Keynes's Influence on Theory and Public Policy', Knopf,
     1947, p. 72.
40   Beveridge, 'Full Employment in a Free Society', p. 248.
41   'Social Insurance and Allied Services', Cmd 6404, HMSO, 1942, para.445.
42   J.M. Keynes, 'Essays in Persuasion', Harcourt, Brace (1931), 1932, p. vii.
43   Galbraith, 'The Affluent Society', p. 212.
44   Galbraith, 'Economics and the Public Purpose', p. x.
45   Galbraith, 'The New Industrial State', pp. 347-8.
46   'Social Insurance and Allied Services', para. 447.
47   Galbraith, 'The Affluent Society', p. 105.
48   Ibid., p. 265.
49   Galbraith, 'Economics and the Public Purpose', p. 162.

50 Ibid., p. 183.
51 Ibid., p. 187.
52 Beveridge, 'Full Employment in a Free Society', p. 37.
53 Ibid., p. 23.
54 Keynes, 'The End of Laissez-Faire', pp. 52-3.
55 Harris, 'John Maynard Keynes', p. ix.
56 J.K. Galbraith, 'American Capitalism' (1952), Penguin, 1963, p. 194.
57 Harris, 'John Maynard Keynes', p. 77.
58 Beveridge, 'Full Employment in a Free Society', p. 206.
59 Galbraith, 'American Capitalism', p. 185.
60 Galbraith, 'The New Industrial State', p. 19.
61 R.L. Heilbroner, 'Between Capitalism and Socialism', Random House, 1970, pp. 230-1.
62 'Guardian', 5 April 1974.
63 Harrod, op. cit., p. 192.
64 R. Lekachman, 'The Age of Keynes' (1966), Penguin, 1969, p. 46.
65 P.M. Sweezy, Keynes the Economist, in S.E. Harris (ed.), 'The New Economics − Keynes's Influence on Theory and Public Policy', p. 108.
66 Galbraith, 'Economics and the Public Purpose', p. 221.
67 Beveridge, 'Why I am a Liberal', p. 8.
68 Beveridge, 'Full Employment in a Free Society', p. 36.
69 A. Smithies, Full Employment in a Free Society, 'American Economic Review', vol. 35, 1945, p. 366.
70 Keynes, 'The End of Laissez-Faire', pp. 46-7.
71 Galbraith, 'American Capitalism', p. 94.
72 Keynes, 'The General Theory . . . .', p. 380.
73 Beveridge, 'Full Employment in a Free Society', p. 29.
74 Ibid., p. 135.
75 Ibid., pp. 181-3.
76 Ibid., p. 186.
77 Stewart, op. cit., pp. 126-7.
78 Keynes, 'The General Theory . . . .', p. 373.
79 Beveridge, 'Full Employment in a Free Society', p. 201.
80 Galbraith, 'Economics and the Public Purpose', p. 213.
81 Beveridge, 'Full Employment in a Free Society', p. 186.
82 Beveridge, 'Why I am a Liberal', p. 37.
83 Beveridge, 'Voluntary Action', p. 319.
84 'Social Insurance and Allied Services', para. 440.
85 Galbraith, 'Economics and the Public Purpose', p. 262.
86 Ibid., p. 263.
87 Beveridge, 'Full Employment in a Free Society', p. 170.
88 Beveridge, 'The Pillars of Security', p. 182.
89 Galbraith, 'The New Industrial State', p. 362.
90 Galbraith, 'Economics and the Public Purpose', pp. 290-1.
91 Harrod, op. cit., p. 399.
92 Ibid., p. 535.
93 Beveridge, 'The Pillars of Security', p. 101.
94 Beveridge, 'Full Employment in a Free Society', p. 254.
95 Churchill, op. cit., p. 82.
96 'Social Insurance and Allied Services', para. 17.
97 Beveridge, 'Full Employment in a Free Society', p. 187.
98 'Social Insurance and Allied Services', para. 244.
99 Galbraith, 'Economics and the Public Purpose', pp. 252-3.
100 'Social Insurance and Allied Services', paras 21, 274.

101 Beveridge, 'The Pillars of Security', p. 134.
102 'Social Insurance and Allied Services', para. 421.
103 Ibid., para. 308.
104 Ibid., para. 9.
105 Ibid., para. 302.
106 Ibid., para. 304.
107 Beveridge, 'Full Employment in a Free Society', p. 256.
108 'Social Insurance and Allied Services', para. 22.
109 Beveridge, 'Full Employment in a Free Society', p. 163.
110 'Social Insurance and Allied Services', para. 442.
111 Galbraith, 'The Affluent Society', pp. 211-12.
112 Galbraith, 'Economics and the Public Purpose', p. 279.
113 Galbraith, 'The Affluent Society', p. 265.

Chapter 4   The Fabian socialists

1 C.A.R. Crosland, 'The Future of Socialism', Cape (1956), 1961, p. 113.
2 R.H.S. Crossman (ed.), 'New Fabian Essays', Turnstile Press, 1952, p. 69.
3 R.H. Tawney, 'The Attack and Other Papers', Allen & Unwin, 1953, p. 182.
4 J.M. Winter and D.M. Joslin, 'R.H. Tawney's Commonplace Book', Cambridge University Press, 1972, p. 54.
5 R.H. Tawney, 'Equality', Allen & Unwin (1931), 1964, p. 27.
6 R.M. Titmuss, Social Welfare and the Art of Giving in E. Fromm (ed.), 'Socialist Humanism', Allen Lane, 1967, pp. 358-9.
7 Crosland, 'The Future of Socialism', p. 196.
8 Ibid., p. 207.
9 Tawney, 'Equality', pp. 27, 107.
10 Crosland, 'The Future of Socialism', p. 215.
11 D. Jay, 'Socialism in the New Society', Longmans, 1962, p. 5.
12 Crosland, 'The Future of Socialism', p. 208.
13 Ibid., p. 210.
14 Tawney, 'Equality', p. 81.
15 Ibid., p. 103.
16 Ibid., pp. 103-4.
17 Crosland, 'The Future of Socialism', p. 237.
18 Tawney, 'Equality', pp. 107-8.
19 Crosland, 'The Future of Socialism', p. 235.
20 Tawney, 'Equality', p. 113.
21 Crosland, 'The Future of Socialism', p. 217.
22 Jay, op. cit., p. 7.
23 Crosland, 'The Future of Socialism', p. 218.
24 A. Crosland, 'Socialism Now', Cape, 1974, pp. 273-4.
25 Crosland, 'The Future of Socialism', p. 295.
26 Ibid., p. 296.
27 Tawney, 'Equality', p. 28.
28 Crosland, 'Socialism Now', pp. 16-17.
29 Crosland, 'The Future of Socialism', p. 217.
30 Winter and Joslin, op. cit., p. 22.
31 Crosland, 'Socialism Now', p. 50.
32 R.H. Tawney, 'The Radical Tradition', Penguin (1964), 1966, p. 169.
33 S.H. Beer, 'Modern British Politics', Faber, 1969, p. 128.
34 R.H. Tawney, 'The Acquisitive Society' (1921), Fontana, 1961, p. 33.
35 Ibid., p. 48.

36 Ibid.
37 Winter and Joslin, op. cit., p. 24.
38 Crosland, 'The Future of Socialism', p. 203.
39 R.M. Titmuss, 'Commitment to Welfare', Allen & Unwin, 1968, p. 151.
40 Ibid., p. 199.
41 Tawney, 'The Radical Tradition', pp. 178-9.
42 E.F.M. Durbin, 'The Politics of Democratic Socialism' (1940), Routledge
     & Kegan Paul, 1957, p. 235.
43 I. Howe (ed.), 'A Handbook of Socialist Thought', Gollancz, 1972, pp.783-4.
44 Crosland, 'Socialism Now', pp. 122-3.
45 Tawney, 'The Acquisitive Society', pp. 149-50.
46 R.M. Titmuss, 'Essays on the Welfare State', Allen & Unwin (1958),
     1964, p. 216.
47 Ibid., p. 239.
48 Winter and Joslin, op. cit., pp. 64-5.
49 Ibid., pp. 12-13.
50 Crosland, 'The Future of Socialism', pp. 94-5.
51 C.A.R. Crosland, 'The Conservative Enemy', Cape, 1962, p. 12.
52 Crosland, 'Socialism Now', p. 71.
53 Titmuss, 'Commitment to Welfare', p. 114.
54 Crossman (ed.), 'New Fabian Essays', p. 42.
55 Crosland, 'The Future of Socialism', pp. 62-5.
56 Crosland, 'Socialism Now', p. 17.
57 Tawney, 'The Attack and Other Papers', p. 170.
58 Quoted in S. Haseler, 'The Gaitskellites', Macmillan, 1969, p. 94.
59 Tawney, 'The Acquisitive Society', pp. 31-2.
60 Titmuss, 'Essays on the Welfare State', p. 238.
61 Tawney, 'The Acquisitive Society', p. 38.
62 Crosland, 'The Future of Socialism', pp. 208 et seq.
63 Titmuss, 'Commitment to Welfare', p. 150.
64 Crosland, 'Socialism Now', pp. 48-9.
65 Tawney, 'Equality', p. 196.
66 Tawney, 'The Acquisitive Society', p. 177.
67 Crosland, 'The Future of Socialism', p. 116.
68 Crosland, 'Socialism Now', pp. 23-4.
69 Titmuss, 'Essays on the Welfare State', p. 242.
70 Tawney, 'The Acquisitive Society', pp. 75-6.
71 Tawney, 'Equality', p. 206.
72 Crosland, 'The Future of Socialism', pp. 26 et seq.
73 Tawney, 'The Radical Tradition', p. 172.
74 Crosland, 'Socialism Now', p. 34.
75 Tawney, 'The Acquisitive Society', p. 180.
76 Crosland, 'Socialism Now', p. 44.
77 Tawney, 'The Acquisitive Society', p. 125.
78 Crosland, 'Socialism Now', p. 42.
79 Tawney, 'The Radical Tradition', p. 174.
80 Crosland, 'The Future of Socialism', p. 113.
81 Crosland, 'The Conservative Enemy', p. 123.
82 Tawney, 'The Attack and Other Papers', p. 97.
83 Tawney, 'Equality', p. 233.
84 Crosland, 'Socialism Now', p. 130.
85 Ibid., p. 74.
86 Ibid., pp. 48-9, 83.

87 Crosland, 'The Future of Socialism', p. 86.
88 Crosland, 'Socialism Now', p. 71.
89 Tawney, 'Equality', p. 125.
90 T.H. Marshall, 'Sociology at the Crossroads', Heinemann, 1963, p. 302.
91 Titmuss, 'Commitment to Welfare ', p. 191.
92 Crosland, 'Socialism Now', p. 194.
93 Titmuss, 'Commitment to Welfare', p. 63.
94 Titmuss, 'Essays on the Welfare State', p. 107.
95 Ibid., pp. 117-18.
96 R.M. Titmuss, 'The Gift Relationship', Allen & Unwin, 1970, p. 225.
97 Crosland, 'The Future of Socialism', p. 148.
98 T.H. Marshall, 'Social Policy', Hutchinson (1965), 3rd ed. 1970, p. 173.
99 Marshall, 'Sociology at the Crossroads', p. 107.
100 Crosland, 'The Future of Socialism', p. 156.
101 Tawney, 'Equality', p. 122.
102 Crosland, 'The Future of Socialism', pp. 164-5.
103 E.g. 'The Future of Socialism', p. 148, 'Socialism Now', p. 71.
104 Crosland, 'The Future of Socialism', p. 262.
105 Crosland, 'The Conservative Enemy', p. 182.
106 Tawney, 'Equality', p.24.
107 Titmuss, 'Essays on the Welfare State', p. 55.
108 Titmuss, 'The Gift Relationship', p. 234.
109 Titmuss, 'Essays on the Welfare State', pp. 73-4.
110 Titmuss, 'Commitment to Welfare', p. 183.
111 Titmuss, 'Essays on the Welfare State', p. 218.
112 Ibid., p. 239.
113 T.H. Marshall, Value Problems of Welfare Capitalism, 'Journal of Social Policy', vol. 1, no. 1, 1972, p. 23.
114 R. Titmuss, Goals of To-day's Welfare State, in P. Anderson and R. Blackburn (eds), "Towards Socialism', Fontana, 1965, p. 357.
115 Crosland, 'The Future of Socialism', pp. 145-6.
116 Ibid., p. 95.
117 Ibid., p. 165.
118 Crosland, 'Socialism Now', p. 21.
119 Titmuss, 'Commitment to Welfare', p. 122.
120 Winter and Joslin, op. cit., p. 13.
121 Titmuss, 'Commitment to Welfare', p. 164.
122 Tawney, 'Equality', p. 148.
123 Ibid., pp. 105-6.
124 Winter and Joslin, op. cit., p. 52.
125 R.M. Titmuss, 'Income Distribution and Social Change', Allen & Unwin, 1965, p. 188.
126 Titmuss, Goals of To-day's Welfare State, p. 362.
127 Titmuss, 'Income Distribution and Social Change', p. 188.
128 Crosland, 'Socialism Now', pp. 45-7.
129 Tawney, 'Equality', p. 40.
130 Crosland, 'The Future of Socialism', pp. 115-16.
131 Crosland, 'Socialism Now', pp. 71-2.
132 E.g. ibid., p. 15.
133 Tawney, 'Equality', p. 120.
134 Ibid., p. 219.
135 Crosland, 'Socialism Now', pp. 22-3.
136 Marshall, 'Sociology at the Crossroads', p. 122.

Chapter 5   The Marxists

1   F.A. Hayek, 'Individualism and Economic Order', Routledge & Kegan Paul, 1949, p. 1.
2   E. Carr, 'The New Society', Macmillan, 1951, p. 16.
3   H. Laski, 'A Grammar of Politics', Allen & Unwin, 1925, p. 142.
4   Ibid., p. 143.
5   Ibid., p. 149.
6   Ibid., p. 150.
7   H. Laski, 'Reflections on the Revolution of our Time', Allen & Unwin, 1943, p. 316.
8   H. Laski, 'Liberty in the Modern State', Allen & Unwin, 3rd ed., 1948, p. 32.
9   J. Strachey, 'The Theory and Practice of Socialism', Gollancz, 1936, p. 198.
10   Ibid., p. 202.
11   Laski, 'A Grammar of Politics', p. 162.
12   Ibid., p. 153.
13   Ibid., p. 154.
14   Ibid., p. 157.
15   Ibid., p. 190.
16   Ibid., p. 194.
17   Ibid.
18   Ibid., p. 195.
19   Ibid.
20   Ibid., p. 199.
21   Strachey, 'The Theory and Practice of Socialism', p. 95.
22   Communist Party of Great Britain, 'People Before Profits', 1970, pp. 11, 13.
23   A. Arblaster, Liberal Values and Socialist Values, 'Socialist Register', Merlin Press, 1972, p. 102.
24   J. Strachey, 'Contemporary Capitalism', Gollancz, 1957, p. 11.
25   Ibid., p. 13.
26   H. Laski, 'The State in Theory and Practice', Allen & Unwin, 1934, p. 108.
27   Ibid., p. 121.
28   Strachey, 'The Theory and Practice of Socialism', p. 403.
29   Laski, 'The State in Theory and Practice', p. 127.
30   R. Miliband, 'The State in Capitalist Society', Weidenfeld & Nicolson, 1969, p. 12.
31   P. Baran and P. Sweezy, 'Monopoly Capital', Penguin, 1970, p. 40.
32   Miliband, 'The State in Capitalist Society', p. 35.
33   Ibid., pp. 66-7.
34   Laski, 'The State in Theory and Practice', p. 118.
35   Laski, 'The State in Capitalist Society', p. 328.
36   Laski, 'The State in Theory and Practice', p. 113.
37   Strachey, 'The Theory and Practice of Socialism', p. 417.
38   R. Miliband, 'Parliamentary Socialism', Allen & Unwin, 1961.
39   J. Saville in 'Knowledge and Beliefs in Politics' ed. R. Benwick et al., Allen & Unwin, 1973, p. 215.
40   Laski, 'The State in Theory and Practice', p. 114.
41   Ibid., p. 121.
42   Ibid., pp. 293-4.
43   Laski, 'Liberty in the Modern State', p. 33.
44   Laski, 'The State in Theory and Practice', p. 213.
45   Strachey, 'The Theory and Practice of Socialism', p. 418.
46   Strachey, 'Contemporary Capitalism', p. 276.

47 Ibid., p. 277.
48 Communist Party of Great Britain, 'The British Road to Socialism', 3rd ed., 1968, p. 17.
49 B. Warren, The Programme of the Communist Party of Great Britain – A Critique, 'New Left Review', no. 63, September-October 1970.
50 Laski, 'The State in Theory and Practice', p. 283.
51 Laski, 'Reflections on the Revolution of our Time', p. 362.
52 Miliband, 'The State in Capitalist Society', pp. 276-7.
53 Strachey, 'Contemporary Capitalism', p. 294.
54 Ibid., p. 188.
55 Laski, 'Liberty in the Modern State', p. 26.
56 Strachey, 'Contemporary Capitalism', p. 180.
57 Laski, 'Reflections on the Revolution of our Time', p. 306.
58 Miliband, 'The State in Capitalist Society', p. 269.
59 Laski, 'A Grammar of Politics', p. 163.
60 Ibid., p. 202.
61 Communist Party of Great Britain, 'People Before Profits', p. 9.
62 Laski, 'Reflections on the Revolution of our Time', p. 331.
63 Ibid.
64 Ibid.
65 Ibid., p. 332.
66 Ibid., p. 331.
67 Ibid., p. 333.
68 Ibid., p. 341.
69 Ibid., p. 357.
70 Ibid., p. 356.
71 J. Gollan, 'The Case for Socialism in the Sixties', 1966, quoted in S. Kissin's 'Communists: All Revisionists Now', Fabian Research Series, no. 299, 1972, p. 35.
72 Ibid., p. 79.
73 Laski, 'The State in Theory and Practice', p. 270.
74 Laski, 'Reflections on the Revolution of our Time', p. 338.
75 Miliband, 'The State in Capitalist Society', p. 271.
76 Laski, 'The State in Theory and Practice', p. 143.
77 Miliband, 'The State in Capitalist Society', pp. 109-10.
78 Ibid., p. 271.
79 M. Barratt Brown, The Welfare State in Britain, 'Socialist Register', Merlin Press, 1971, pp. 202-3.
80 Strachey, 'Contemporary Capitalism', pp. 150-1.
81 J. Strachey, 'What Are We To Do?', Gollancz, 1938, p. 354.
82 Laski, 'The State in Theory and Practice', p. 79.
83 Strachey, 'Contemporary Capitalism', p. 283.
84 Communist Party of Great Britain, 'People Before Profits', p. 12.
85 M. Rossdale, A Socialist Health Service, 'New Left Review', no. 34, November-December 1965.
86 J.C. Kincaid, 'Poverty and Equality in Britain', Penguin, 1973, p. 235.
87 R. Miliband, in 'Poverty, Inequality and Class Structure', ed. D. Wedderburn, Cambridge University Press, 1974, p. 194.
88 M. Barratt Brown, op. cit., p. 194.

Chapter 6   Social justice and social policy

1 'National Health Service: Twentieth Anniversary Conference', HMSO,

1968, p. 10.

2   'Eighth Report from the Expenditure Committee', Session 1971-2, HC 515, HMSO 1972, Appendix 4.

3   'Health Services Financing' (a report commissioned in 1967 by the British Medical Association, n.d.), p. 235.

4   'Health and Personal Social Service Statistics for England 1973', HMSO, 1973, Tables 4. 10 and 4. 11.

5   A. Maynard, Inequalities in Psychiatric Care in England and Wales, 'Social Science and Medicine', vol. 6, 1972, p. 223.

6   J.R. Butler, J.M. Bevan and R.C. Taylor, 'Family Doctors and Public Policy', Routledge & Kegan Paul, 1973, pp. 28-9.

7   Ibid., pp. 40-2.

8   'Health and Personal Social Service Statistics for England 1973', Table 3.28.

9   P.J. Cook and R.O. Walker, The Geographical Distribution of Dental Care in the United Kingdom, 'British Dental Journal', vol. 122, 1967, p. 445.

10 Institute of Municipal Treasurers and Accountants and Society of County Treasurers, 'Local Health Service Statistics 1952-3', and 'Local Health and Social Service Statistics 1971-2', 1953 and 1973.

11 P. Draper, M. Kogan and J.N. Morris, 'The National Health Service: Three Views', Fabian Research Series 287, 1970, p. 5.

12 B.E. Coates and E.M. Rawstron, 'Regional Variations in Britain', Batsford, 1971, p. 242.

13 'Hospital Costing Returns', HMSO, 1973.

14 Institute of Municipal Treasurers and Accountants and Society of County Treasurers, 'Education Statistics 1952-3', 1954.

15 Chartered Institute of Public Finance and Accountancy and the Society of County Treasurers, 'Education Statistics 1972-3', 1973.

16 D.S. Byrne and W. Williamson, Some Intra-Regional Variations in Educational Provision and Their Bearing upon Educational Attainment – the case of the North East in J. Raynor and J. Harden, 'Equality and City Schools', Routledge & Kegan Paul, 1973, p. 133.

17 C. Jencks, 'Inequality', Allen Lane, 1973, p. 29.

18 R. Davie, N. Butler and H. Goldstein, 'From Birth to Seven', Longman, 1972, p. 102.

19 J.W.B. Douglas, 'The Home and the School', Panther, 1968, p. 76.

20 H. Glennerster, Education and Inequality in P. Townsend and N. Bosanquet, 'Labour and Inequality', Fabian, 1972, p. 91.

21 'Statistics of Education 1972', vol. I, HMSO, 1973, Table 10.

22 'Children and Their Primary Schools', HMSO, 1967, para. 151.

23 Ibid., para. 169.

24 C. Benn and B. Simon, 'Half Way There', McGraw-Hill, 1970, p. 350.

25 Glennerster, op. cit., p. 104.

26 'Educational Priority', vol. I., HMSO, 1972, p. 6.

27 Cf. 'Guardian', 4 September 1974 for recent proposals to raise allowances and reduce the anomalies.

28 'Wealth Tax', Cmnd 5704, HMSO, 1974, p. 25.

29 A.B. Atkinson, 'Unequal Shares', Penguin, 1974, p. 22.

30 'Widening the Choice: The Next Steps in Housing', Cmnd 5280, HMSO, 1973, p. 1.

31 'Social Trends', no. 4, HMSO, 1973, p. 155.

32 'The General Household Survey', HMSO, 1973, p. 131.

33 Ibid., p. 126.

34 Ibid., p. 125.

35 'Social Trends', no. 4, p. 160.
36 'New Society', 15 August 1974.
37 National and Local Government Officers Association, 'Housing: The Way Ahead', 1973, p. 9.
38 R. Klein et al., 'Social Policy and Public Expenditure 1974', Centre for Studies in Social Policy, 1974, p. 51.
39 H.L. Wilensky and C.N. Lebeaux, 'Industrial Society and Social Welfare', Free Press, 1965, p. 42.
40 'Guardian', 1 February 1974.
41 R.M. Titmuss, 'Essays on the Welfare State', Allen & Unwin, 1958, p. 52.
42 J. Greve, D. Page and S. Greve, 'Homeless in London', Scottish Academic Press, 1971, p. 86.
43 R.A. Pinker, 'Social Theory and Social Policy', Heinemann, 1971, p. 201.
44 'Strategy for Pensions', Cmnd 4755, HMSO, 1971, para, 87.
45 G.V. Rimlinger, Social Security in the United States and the U.S.S.R. in M. Zald, 'Social Welfare Institutions', Wiley, 1965, p. 107.
46 Pinker, op. cit., p. 90.
47 R.A. Pinker, 'The Welfare State', Bookstall Publications, 1973, p. 22.
48 M. Wynn, 'Family Policy', Michael Joseph, 1970, p. 233.
49 'Social Insurance and Allied Services', Cmd 6404, HMSO, 1942, para. 21.
50 Pinker, 'Social Theory and Social Policy', p. 142.
51 Quoted in C.A.R. Crosland, 'The Conservative Enemy', Cape, 1962, p. 18.
52 J.M. Romanyshyn, 'Social Welfare: Charity to Justice', Random House, 1971, p. 40.
53 T.H. Marshall, Value Problems of Welfare Capitalism, 'Journal of Social Policy', vol. 1, no. 1, 1972, p. 29.
54 R.H. Tawney, 'Equality', Allen & Unwin, 1964, p. 103.
55 'Children and Their Primary Schools', HMSO, 1967, para. 152.
56 A.L. Webb and J.E.B. Sieve, 'Income Redistribution and the Welfare State', Occasional Papers on Social Administration, no. 41, Bell, 1971, p.12.
57 M. Meacher, The Coming Class Struggle, 'New Statesman', 4 January 1974, p. 7.
58 Quoted in A.B. Atkinson, The Reform of Wealth Taxes in Britain in B. Crick and W.A. Robson, 'Taxation Policy', Penguin, 1973, p. 103.
59 J.C. Kincaid, 'Poverty and Equality in Britain', Penguin, 1973, p. 109.
60 Meacher, op. cit.
61 Jencks, op. cit., pp. 8-9.
62 J. Rawls, 'A Theory of Justice', Oxford University Press, 1972, p. 3.
63 Ibid., p. 303.
64 Ibid., pp. 14-15.
65 W.G. Runciman, 'Relative Deprivation and Social Justice', Routledge & Kegan Paul, 1966, p. 273.
66 Rawls, op. cit., p. 101.
67 Ibid., pp. 100-1.
68 J. Bradshaw, A Taxonomy of Social Need in 'Problems and Progress in Medical Care', ed. G. McLachlan, Oxford University Press, 1972, p. 73.
69 R. Walton, Need: A Central Concept, 'Social Service Quarterly', vol. 43, 1969.
70 A, Forder, 'Concepts in Social Administration', Routledge & Kegan Paul, 1974, p. 48.
71 D. Harvey, 'Social Justice and the City', Arnold, 1973, p. 165.
72 Jencks, op. cit., p. 232.

FuRTHER REAdiNG

Crosland, C.A.R., 'The Future of Socialism' (Cape paperback, 1956) (although
twenty years old it remains the classic statement of the 'revisionist' Labour
approach).

Friedman, M., 'Capitalism and Freedom' (Phoenix Books, 1962) (a brief and
very readable statement of Friedman's philosophy).

Galbraith, J.K., 'Economics and the Public Purpose' (Penguin, 1975) (the most
recent statement in Galbraith's ongoing analysis of contemporary society).

Hayek, F.A., 'The Constitution of Liberty' (Routledge & Kegan Paul, 1960)
(perhaps the most stimulating of Hayek's works).

Laski, H., 'The State in Theory and Practice' (Allen & Unwin, 1934) (a good
introduction to Laski's ideas).

Miliband, R., 'The State in Capitalist Society' (Quartet Books, 1973) (essentially
an analysis of power but valuable for a general understanding of the
Marxist perspective).

Tawney, R.H., 'The Acquisitive Society' (Fontana, 1961) (Tawney's statement
of his basic social philosophy).

Titmuss, R.M., 'The Gift Relationship' (Penguin, 1973) (probably the most
useful of the author's books for providing insights into his social philosophy).

The books have been listed in their most accessible editions. All except Hayek
and Laski are paperbacks.

Bibliography

Anderson, P. and Blackburn, R. (eds), 'Towards Socialism', Fontana, 1965.
Arblaster, A., Liberal Values and Socialist Values, 'Socialist Register', Merlin Press, 1972.
Ashton, T.S., Richard Henry Tawney 1880-1962, 'Proceedings of the British Academy', vol. XLVIII, 1962.
Atkinson, A.B., 'Unequal Shares', Penguin, 1974.
Baran, P. and Sweezy, P., 'Monopoly Capital', Penguin, 1970.
Barratt Brown, M., The Welfare State in Britain, 'Socialist Register', Merlin Press, 1971.
Beer, S.H., 'Modern British Politics', Faber, 1969.
Bell, D., 'The End of Ideology', Free Press, 1960.
Bell, D., 'The Coming of Post Industrial Society', Basic Books, 1973.
Benn, C. and Simon, B., 'Half Way There', McGraw-Hill, 1970.
Benwick, R. et al. (ed.), 'Knowledge and Beliefs in Politics', Allen & Unwin, 1973.
Beveridge, W.H., 'The Pillars of Security', Macmillan (New York), 1943.
Beveridge, W.H., 'Full Employment in a Free Society', Allen & Unwin, 1944.
Beveridge, W.H., 'Why I am a Liberal', Jenkins, 1945.
Beveridge, W.H., 'Voluntary Action', Allen & Unwin, 1948.
Beveridge, W.H., 'Power and Influence', Hodder & Stoughton, 1953.
Birnbaum, N., 'The Crisis of Industrial Society', Oxford University Press, 1969.
Bottomore, T.B., 'Elites and Society', Pitman, 1964.
Boyson, R. (ed.), 'Right Turn', Churchill Press, 1970.
British Medical Association, 'Health Services Financing', n.d.
Butler, J.R., Bevan, J.M. and Taylor, R.C., 'Family Doctors and Public Policy', Routledge & Kegan Paul, 1973.
Carr, E., 'The New Society', Macmillan, 1951.
Chartered Institute of Public Finance and Accountancy and the Society of County Treasurers, 'Education Statistics 1972-3', 1973.
Churchill, W.S., 'Liberalism and the Social Problem', Hodder & Stoughton, 1909.
Coates, B.E. and Rawstron, E.M., 'Regional Variations in Britain', Batsford, 1971.
Communist Party of Great Britain, 'The British Road to Socialism', 3rd ed. 1968.
Communist Party of Great Britain, 'People Before Profits', 1970.

Cook, P.J. and Walker, R.O., The Geographical Distribution of Dental Care in the United Kingdom, 'British Dental Journal', vol. 122, 1967.

Coser, L., 'The Functions of Social Conflict', Routledge & Kegan Paul, 1956.

Crick, B. and Robson, W.A., 'Taxation Policy', Penguin, 1973.

Crosland, C.A.R., 'The Future of Socialism', Cape, 1956.

Crosland, C.A.R., 'The Conservative Enemy', Cape, 1962.

Crosland, A., 'Socialism Now', Cape, 1974.

Crossman, R.H.S. (ed.), 'New Fabian Essays', Turnstile Press, 1952.

Dahl, R.A., 'Social Science Research on Business: Product and Potential', Columbia University Press, 1959.

Dahl, R.A., 'Who Governs?', Yale University Press, 1961.

Dahrendorf, R., 'Class and Class Conflict in Industrial Society', Routledge & Kegan Paul, 1959.

Davie, R., Butler, N. and Goldstein, H., 'From Birth to Seven', Longman, 1972.

Dicey, A.V., 'Law and Public Opinion in England', Macmillan, 1914, 2nd ed., 1962.

Douglas, J.W.B., 'The Home and the School', Panther, 1968.

Draper, P., Kogan, M. and Morris, J.N., 'The National Health Service: Three Views', Fabian Research Series 287, 1970.

Dubin, R., Approaches to the Study of Social Conflict: A Colloquium, 'Conflict Resolution', vol. I, no. 2, 1957.

Durbin, E.F.M., 'The Politics of Democratic Socialism' (1940), Routledge & Kegan Paul, 1957.

Etzioni, A. and E. (eds), 'Social Change', Basic Books, 1964.

Fisher, F.J., Titmuss, R.M. and Williams, J.R., 'R.H. Tawney, A Portrait by Several Hands', LSE, 1960.

Forder, A., 'Concepts in Social Administration', Routledge & Kegan Paul, 1974.

Friedman, M., 'Capitalism and Freedom', University of Chicago Press, 1962.

Fromm, E. (ed.), 'Socialist Humanism', Allen Lane, 1967.

Galbraith, J.K., 'American Capitalism' (1952), Penguin, 1963.

Galbraith, J.K., 'The New Industrial State', Deutsch, 1967.

Galbraith, J.K., 'The Affluent Society', Penguin, 2nd ed., 1970.

Galbraith, J.K., 'Economics and the Public Purpose', Deutsch, 1974.

Goldthorpe, J.H., The Development of Social Policy in England 1800-1914, 'Transactions of the Fifth World Congress of Sociology', vol. 4, no. 4, 1962.

Gouldner, A.W., 'The Coming Crisis of Western Sociology', Heinemann, 1971.

Greve, J., Page, D. and Greve, S., 'Homeless in London', Scottish Academic Press, 1971.

Harris, S.E., 'John Maynard Keynes', Scribner's, 1955.

Harris, S.E. (ed.), 'The New Economics – Keynes's Influence on Theory and Public Policy', Knopf, 1947.

Harrod, R.F., 'The Life of John Maynard Keynes', Macmillan, 1951.

Harvey, D., 'Social Justice and the City', Arnold, 1973.

Haseler, S., 'The Gaitskellites', Macmillan, 1969.

Hayek, F.A., 'The Road to Serfdom', Routledge, 1944.

Hayek, F.A., 'Individualism and Economic Order', Routledge & Kegan Paul, 1949.

Hayek, F.A., 'The Constitution of Liberty', Routledge & Kegan Paul, 1960.

Hayek, F.A., 'Law, Legislation and Liberty', vol. I, Routledge & Kegan Paul, 1973.

Heilbroner, R.L., 'Between Capitalism and Socialism', Random House, 1970.

HMSO, 'Social Insurance and Allied Services', Cmd 6404, 1942.

HMSO, 'Children and Their Primary Schools', 1967.

HMSO, 'National Health Service: Twentieth Anniversary Conference', 1968.

HMSO, 'Strategy for Pensions', Cmnd 4755, 1971.

HMSO, 'Educational Priority', vol. I, 1972.

HMSO, 'Eighth Report from the Expenditure Committee', 1971-2, HC 515, 1972.
HMSO, 'The General Household Survey', 1973.
HMSO, 'Health and Personal Social Service Statistics for England 1973', 1973.
HMSO, 'Hospital Costing Returns', 1973.
HMSO, 'Social Trends', no. 4, 1973.
HMSO, 'Statistics of Education 1972', vol I, 1973.
HMSO, 'Widening the Choice: The Next Steps in Housing', Cmnd 5280, 1973.
HMSO, 'Wealth Tax', Cmnd 5704, 1974.
Horton, J., Order and Conflict Theories of Social Problems as Competing Ideologies, 'American Journal of Sociology', vol. 71, no. 6, May 1966.
Howe, I. (ed.), 'A Handbook of Socialist Thought', Gollancz, 1972.
Hutchinson, T.W., 'Half a Century of Hobarts', Institute of Economic Affairs, 1970.
Inkeles, A., 'What is Sociology? An Introduction to the Discipline and Profession', Prentice-Hall, 1964.
Institute of Municipal Treasurers and Accountants and Society of County Treasurers, 'Local Health Service Statistics 1952-3', 1953.
Institute of Municipal Treasurers and Accountants and Society of County Treasurers, 'Education Statistics 1952-3', 1954.
Institute of Municipal Treasurers and Accountants and Society of County Treasurers, 'Local Health and Social Service Statistics 1971-2', 1973.
Jay, D., 'Socialism in the New Society', Longmans, 1962.
Jencks, C., 'Inequality', Allen Lane, 1973.
Kerr, C. et al., 'Industrialism and Industrial Man', Harvard University Press, 1960.
Keynes, J.M., 'The End of Laissez-Faire', Hogarth, 1926.
Keynes, J.M., 'Essays in Persuasion', Harcourt, Brace, 1931.
Keynes, J.M., 'The General Theory of Employment, Interest and Money', Macmillan, 1936.
Kincaid, J.C., 'Poverty and Equality in Britain', Penguin, 1973.
Kissin, S., 'Communists: All Revisionists Now', Fabian Research Series, no. 299, 1972.
Klein, R. et al., 'Social Policy and Public Expenditure 1974', Centre for Studies in Social Policy, 1974.
Laski, H., 'A Grammar of Politics', Allen & Unwin, 1925.
Laski, H., 'The State in Theory and Practice', Allen & Unwin, 1934.
Laski, H., 'Reflections on the Revolution of our Time', Allen & Unwin, 1943.
Laski, H., 'Liberty in the Modern State', Allen & Unwin, 3rd ed., 1948.
Lees, D.S., 'Health through Choice', Institute of Economic Affairs, 1961.
Lejeune, A. (ed.), 'Enoch Powell', Stacey, 1970.
Lekachman, R., 'The Age of Keynes' (1966), Penguin, 1969.
Lockwood, D., Some Remarks on 'The Social System', 'British Journal of Sociology', vol. vii, no. 2, 1956.
McLachlan, G. (ed.), 'Problems and Progress in Medical Care', Oxford University Press, 1972.
Macmillan, H., 'Reconstruction: A Plea for a National Policy', Macmillan, 1933.
Macmillan, H., 'The Middle Way', Macmillan, 1938.
Mankoff, M., Power in Advanced Capitalist Society: A Review Essay, 'Social Problems', vol. 17, 1969-70.
Marcuse, H., 'One-Dimensional Man', Routledge & Kegan Paul, 1964.
Marshall, T.H., 'Sociology at the Crossroads', Heinemann, 1963.
Marshall, T.H., 'Social Policy', Hutchinson, 1965.
Marshall, T.H., Value Problems of Welfare Capitalism, 'Journal of Social Policy', vol. 1, no. 1, 1972.
Maynard, A., Inequalities in Psychiatric Care in England and Wales, 'Social

Bibliography

Science and Medicine', vol. 6, 1972.
Meacher, M., The Coming Class Struggle, 'New Statesman', 4 January 1974.
Miliband, R., 'Parliamentary Socialism', Allen & Unwin, 1961.
Miliband, R., 'The State in Capitalist Society', Weidenfeld & Nicolson, 1969.
Mills, C.W., 'The Power Elite', Oxford University Press, 1956.
National and Local Government Officers Association, 'Housing: The Way Ahead', 1973.
Nisbet, R.A. and Merton, R.K., 'Contemporary Social Problems', Harcourt, Brace & World, 1966.
Ortega y Gasset, J., 'History as a System and Other Essays', Norton, 1961.
Parenti, M., The Possibilities for Political Change, 'Politics and Society', vol. 1, no. 1, November 1970.
Parkin, F., 'Class Inequality and Political Order', MacGibbon & Kee, 1971.
Parsons, T., 'Towards a General Theory of Action', Harvard University Press, 1951.
Parsons, T., The Distribution of Power in American Society, 'World Politics', vol. X, no. 1, October 1957.
Parsons, T., 'Sociological Theory and Modern Society', Free Press, 1969.
Perrow, L., The Sociological Perspective and Political Pluralism, 'Social Research', vol. 31, no. 4, Winter 1964.
Pinker, R.A., 'Social Theory and Social Policy', Heinemann, 1971.
Pinker, R.A., 'The Welfare State', Bookstall Publications, 1973.
Powell, E., 'Medicine and Politics', Pitman, 1966.
Powell, E., 'Freedom and Reality', Elliot Right Way Books, 1969.
Powell, E., 'Still to Decide', Elliot Right Way Books, 1972.
Rawls, J., 'A Theory of Justice', Oxford University Press, 1972.
Raynor, J. and Harden, J., 'Equality and City Schools', Routledge & Kegan Paul, 1973.
Rex, J., 'Key Problems of Sociological Theory', Routledge & Kegan Paul, 1961.
Robinson, J., 'Economic Philosophy', Penguin, 1962.
Romanyshyn, J.M., 'Social Welfare: Charity to Justice', Random House, 1971.
Ross, R. and Staines, G.L., The Politics of Analysing Social Problems, 'Social Problems', vol. 20, no. 1, Summer 1972.
Rossdale, M., A Socialist Health Service, 'New Left Review', no. 34, November–December 1965.
Rule, J.R., The Problem With Social Problems, 'Politics and Society', Fall 1971.
Runciman, W.G., 'Relative Deprivation and Social Justice', Routledge & Kegan Paul, 1966.
Ryan, W., 'Blaming the Victim', Orbach & Chambers, 1971.
Sharpe, M.E., 'John Kenneth Galbraith and the Lower Economics', International Arts & Sciences Press, 1973.
Smithies, A., Full Employment in a Free Society, 'American Economic Review', vol. 35, 1945.
Stewart, M., 'Keynes and After', Penguin, 1967.
Strachey, J., 'The Theory and Practice of Socialism', Gollancz, 1936.
Strachey, J., 'What Are We To Do?', Gollancz, 1938.
Strachey, J., 'Contemporary Capitalism', Gollancz, 1957.
Sweezy, P.M., 'Modern Capitalism and Other Essays', Monthly Review Press, 1972.
Sykes, G.M., 'Social Problems in America', Scott, Foresman, 1971.
Tawney, R.H., 'The Acquisitive Society' (1921), Fontana, 1961.
Tawney, R.H., 'Equality', Allen & Unwin, 1931.
Tawney, R.H., 'The Attack and Other Papers', Allen & Unwin, 1953.
Tawney, R.H., 'The Radical Tradition', Penguin, 1964.

Terrill, R., 'R.H.Tawney and his Times', Deutsch, 1974.
Titmuss, R.M., 'Essays on the Welfare State', Allen & Unwin, 1958.
Titmuss, R.M., 'Income Distribution and Social Change', Allen & Unwin, 1965.
Titmuss, R.M., 'Commitment to Welfare', Allen & Unwin, 1968.
Titmuss, R.M., 'The Gift Relationship', Allen & Unwin, 1970.
Titmuss, R.M., 'Social Policy', Allen & Unwin, 1974.
Townsend, P. and Bosanquet, N., 'Labour and Inequality', Fabian, 1972.
Urry, J. and Wakeford, J. (eds), 'Power in Britain', Heinemann, 1973.
Van den Berghe, P.L., Dialectic and Functionalism: Towards a Theoretical
    Synthesis, 'American Sociological Review', vol. 28, no. 5, October 1963.
Walton, R., Need: A Central Concept, 'Social Service Quarterly', vol. 43, 1969.
Warren, B., The Programme of the Communist Party of Great Britain – A
    Critique, 'New Left Review', no. 63, September-October 1970.
Webb, A.L. and Sieve, J.E.B., 'Income Redistribution and the Welfare State',
    Occasional Papers on Social Administration, no. 41, Bell, 1971.
Wedderburn, D. (ed.), 'Poverty, Inequality and Class Structure', Cambridge
    University Press, 1974.
Wilensky, H.L. and Lebeaux, C.N., 'Industrial Society and Social Welfare',
    Free Press, 1965.
Winch, D., 'Economics and Policy', Hodder & Stoughton, 1969.
Winter, J.M. and Joslin, D.M., 'R.H. Tawney's Commonplace Book', Cambridge
    University Press, 1972.
Wynn, M., 'Family Policy', Michael Joseph, 1970.
Zald, M., 'Social Welfare Institutions', Wiley, 1975.

Name index

Subject index